The Complete Welcome Back-to-School Book

by *Beth Button* with *Ellen Sussman*, contributor

illustrated by *Marilynn G. Barr*

Teaching & Learning Company

1204 Buchanan St., P.O. Box 10
Carthage, IL 62321-0010

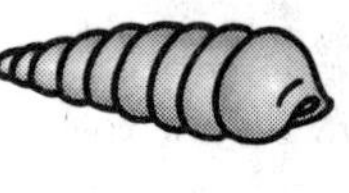

This book belongs to

____

Cover art by Marilynn G. Barr

Copyright © 2001, Teaching & Learning Company

ISBN No. 1-57310-268-7

Printing No. 987654321

Teaching & Learning Company
1204 Buchanan St., P.O. Box 10
Carthage, IL 62321-0010

Table of Contents

Teacher Forms & Letters 7
 A Note from Your Teacher 8
 Introducing . . . Me! 9
 A Note from Your Child's Teacher 10
 Student Information Form 11
 Class Rules 12
 A Call for Volunteers 13
 Our Daily Schedule/Our Weekly Schedule 14
 Attendance/Grade Chart 15
 Daily Lesson Plan .16
 Today's Homework .17
 What's happening in . . . (calendar) 18
 Class News 19
 We're Going on a Feild Trip! 20
 While You Were Out 21
 Useful Information for Substitute Teachers . . .22
 Testing in Progress 23
 Kid Coupons 24
 We Read at My House 25
 Let's Find Out 26
 Teacher Notepaper .27

Theme Units 31
Bugs 32
 The Hall
  Hallway Sign 32
 The Door
  Door Decorations 33
 The Walls
  Class Rules Chart 33
  Playground Rules Chart 34
  Lost-a-Tooth Chart 34
  Job Chart 35
  Math Work Bulletin Board 35
  Student Work Bulletin Board 36
  Story Web Bullentin Board 36
 The Desks
  Folder Label 37
  Desk Name Tag 37
 The Children
  Name Tag 38
  Bus and Field Trip Tag 38
  Locker/Cubby Label 38
 The Awards & Rewards
  Badges, Bookmarks and Bookplates 39
  Certificates 40
 The Handouts
  I Know! I Know! All About Bugs 41
  Eight Facts About Spiders 42
  What Am I? 43
 The Books & Media .44
 The Snacks 45
 The Paper
  Lined Paper 46
  Bordered Paper 47
  Notepaper 48
 The Clip Art 49
 The Reproducibles .51

Sports 66
 The Hall
  Hallway Sign 66
 The Door
  Door Decorations 67
 The Walls
  Class Rules Chart 67
  Meet the Class Bulletin Board 68
  Reading Work Bulletin Board 68
  Math Work Bulletin Board 69
  Class News Bulletin Board 69
 The Desks
  Folder Label 70
  Desk Name Tag 70
 The Children
  Name Tag 71
  Bus and Field Trip Tag 71
  Locker/Cubby Label 71
 The Awards & Rewards
  Badges, Bookmarks and Bookplates 72
  Certificates 73
 The Handouts
  I Know! I Know! All About Sports 74
  Fill-In Sports Card 75
  What's Your Favorite Sport? 76
 The Books & Media .77
 The Snacks 78
 The Paper
  Lined Paper 79
  Bordered Paper 80
  Notepaper 81
 The Clip Art 82
 The Reproducibles .84

Rain Forest 99
  The Door
    Door Decorations 99
  The Walls
    Rain Forest Facts Bulletin Board 100
    Spelling Work Bulletin Board 100
    Today's Weather 101
    Birthday Chart .101
    Rain Forest Alphabet Frieze 102
    Rain Forest Facts 103
  The Desks
    Folder Label 105
    Desk Name Tag 105
  The Children
    Name Tag 106
    Bus and Field Trip Tag 106
    Locker/Cubby Label 106
  The Awards & Rewards
    Badges, Bookmarks and Bookplates 107
    Certificates 108
  The Handouts
    I Know! I Know! All About Rain Forests . . .109
    Rain Forest Hide-and-Seek 110
    The Rain Forest News 111
  The Books & Media 112
  The Snacks 113
  The Paper
    Lined Paper 114
    Bordered Paper 115
    Notepaper 116
  The Clip Art 117
  The Reproducibles 119

Fall 131
  The Door
    Door Decorations 131
  The Windows
    Suncatchers 132
  The Walls
    Learning Path 132
    Ideas Bulletin Board 133
    Reading Bulletin Board 133
    Fall Finds Bulletin Board 134
    Job Chart 134
  The Desks
    Folder Label 135
    Desk Name Tag 135
  The Children
    Name Tag 136
    Bus and Field Trip Tag 136

    Locker/Cubby Label 136
  The Awards & Rewards
    Badges, Bookmarks and Bookplates 137
    Certificates 138
  The Handouts
    I Know! I Know! All About Fall 139
    Fall Leaves 140
    Signs of the Seasons 141
  The Books & Media 142
  The Snacks 143
  The Paper
    Lined Paper 134
    Bordered Paper 145
    Notepaper 146
  The Clip Art 147
  The Reproducibles 149

Sea Creatures 162
  The Door
    Door Decorations 162
  The Windows
    Window Decorations 163
  The Ceiling
    Ceiling Decorations 163
  The Walls
    Sea Life Bulletin Board 164
    Friendship Bulletin Board 164
    Student Work Bulletin Board 165
    Class Rules Chart 165
    I Lost a Tooth Display 165
  The Desks
    Folder Label 166
    Desk Name Tag 166
  The Children
    Name Tag 167
    Bus and Field Trip Tag 167
    Locker/Cubby Label 167
  The Awards & Rewards
    Badges, Bookmarks and Bookplates 168
    Certificates 169
  The Handouts
    I Know! I Know! All About Sea Creatures . .170
    A Puzzle with a "Porpoise" 171
    Take a Look at That! 172
  The Books & Media 173
  The Snacks 174
  The Paper
    Lined Paper 175
    Bordered Paper 176
    Notepaper 177

The Clip Art 179
The Reproducibles 180

Outer Space 193
  The Hall
    Hallway Sign 193
  The Door
    Door Decorations 194
  The Ceiling
    Ceiling Decorations 194
  The Walls
    Reading Bulletin Board 195
    Star of the Week Bulletin Board 195
    Space Mural 196
    Student Work Bulletin Boards 196
    News and Views from Planet Earth 196
  The Desks
    Folder Label 197
    Desk Name Tag 197
  The Children
    Name Tag 198
    Bus and Field Trip Tag 198
    Locker/Cubby Label 198
  The Awards & Rewards
    Badges, Bookmarks and Bookplates 199
    Certificates 200
  The Handouts
    I Know! I Know! All About Outer Space . . .201
    Greetings from Outer Space 202
    The Place We Call Space 203
  The Books & Media 204
  The Snack 205
  The Paper
    Lined Paper 206
    Bordered Paper 207
    Notepaper 208
  The Clip Art 209
  The Reproducibles 211

Classic Tales 225
  The Hall
    Hallway Sign 225
  The Door
    Door Decorations 226
  The Walls
    Student Work Bulletin Board 226
    Math Work Bulletin Board 227
    Safety Rules Bulletin Board 227
    Literature Wall Decorations 228
    Job Chart 228

  The Desks
    Folder Label 229
    Desk Name Tag 229
  The Children
    Name Tag 230
    Bus and Field Trip Tag 230
    Locker/Cubby Label 230
  The Awards & Rewards
    Bookmarks, Bookplates and Certificates . .231
  The Handouts
    I Know! I Know! All About Classic Tales . . .233
    Alice's A-Mazing Adventure 234
    Flying Lessons .235
  The Books & Media 236
  The Snack 237
  The Paper
    Lined Paper 238
    Bordered Paper 239
    Notepaper 240
  The Clip Art 241
  The Reproducibles 243

Dear Teacher or Parent,

For every teacher, whether a veteran or a newcomer to the profession, back-to-school is one of the busiest and most exciting times of the year. We, like our students, approach the start of school full of anticipation. Anxious to try out some fresh teaching ideas, eager to meet a new roomful of children, we wonder where this learning journey will take us.

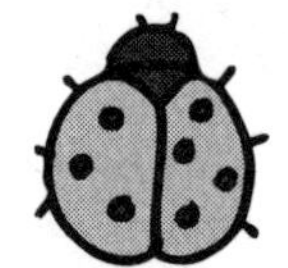

But there's little time for reflection, for most of us feel the pressure rising. There's so much to do! That's where this book comes in. We think you'll find it indispensable, year after year, as a time-saving source for forms and letters, and for establishing a welcoming, stimulating environment from the first day.

The forms in the first section of the book cover back-to-school situations, from getting acquainted with students to communicating with parents, from keeping track of lessons, homework and grades to encouraging and rewarding children's work. You may use the forms and letters "as is," or adapt them to your special needs.

The material in the second section revolves around seven themes: bugs, sports, the rain forest, fall, sea creatures, outer space and classic tales. Within each theme you'll find a variety of ways to set a mood and inspire learning, including door decorations, student work displays, special wall charts, activities, writing papers, desk tags and more. By picking and choosing amoung these adaptable, thematic materials, you can create an inviting space that reflects your personality, your teaching style and your curriculum. From the moment your students step inside, they'll know that your classroom is a warm, creative place, a place where each child is welcome and where learning is valued.

Welcome back!

Beth   *Ellen*

Beth Button & Ellen Sussman

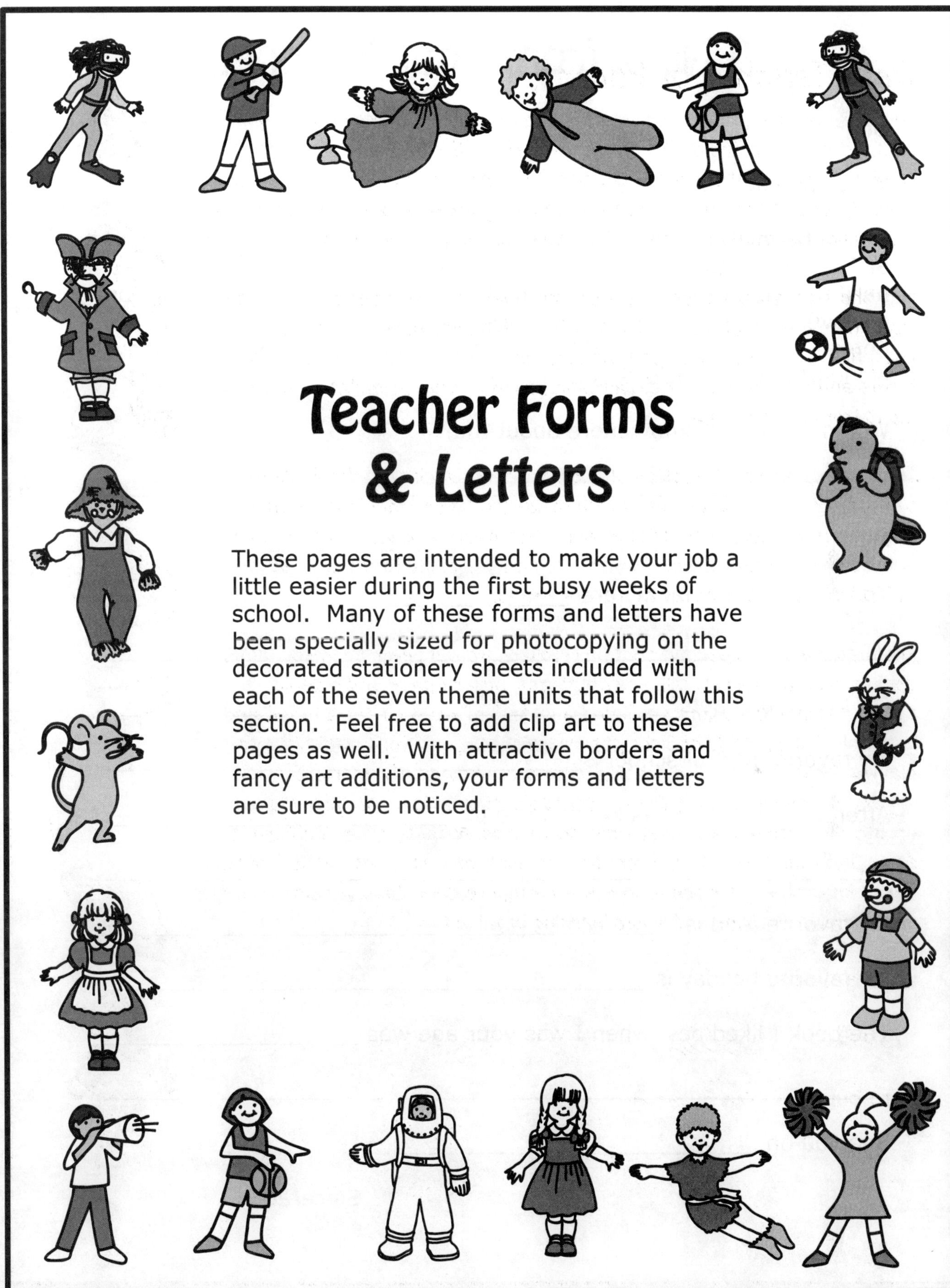

Teacher Forms & Letters

These pages are intended to make your job a little easier during the first busy weeks of school. Many of these forms and letters have been specially sized for photocopying on the decorated stationery sheets included with each of the seven theme units that follow this section. Feel free to add clip art to these pages as well. With attractive borders and fancy art additions, your forms and letters are sure to be noticed.

A Note from Your Teacher

Dear ______________________________,

Welcome back to school!

I'm so happy that school is starting soon, and I hope you are as excited as I am about the learning adventure ahead of us. We're going to work hard this year, but we'll have some fun too, as we explore, observe and discover lots of new things and read many beautiful and interesting books. I'm looking forward to getting to know you and sharing many wonderful experiences together.

Would you like to know more about me?

My name is____.

My birthday is ____.

The people in my family are ___________________________________

____.

Do I have any pets?______________________________________.

My favorite part of school is_______________________________.

After school and on weekends I like to _________________________

____.

My favorite food is _______________________________________.

My favorite holiday is_____________________________________.

The book I liked best when I was your age was ___________________

____.

See you on _______________________________!

Sincerely,

Introducing . . . Me!

My name is _________________________. My nickname is _______________.

I am in _________ grade. My teacher's name is __________________________.

My birthday is _______________________________.

I am _____________ years old.

My eyes are ___________________________. My hair is ____________________________.

The people and pets in my family are _____________________________________

____.

My friends' names are ____.

My favorite book is ____.

My favorite movie is ____.

My favorite food is ____.

My favorite animal is ____.

My favorite color is ____.

My favorite holiday is ____.

My favorite part of school is ____.

After school and on weekends I like to ___________________________________

____.

I want to be a ____ when I grow up.

This is a picture of me.

A Note from Your Child's Teacher

Dear Parents/Guardians,

I'm looking forward to a wonderful year with your children. Here is some information that will help everyone get off to a good start.

School starts at ______________. School ends at ______________.

Snack time ______________ Lunch time ______________ Recess ______________

Phys. Ed. ______________ Music ______________ Art ______________

Library ______________ Other ______________

Please send the items checked below to school with your child.

- ❑ Pencils
- ❑ Erasers
- ❑ Pencil box
- ❑ Crayons, markers
- ❑ Ruler
- ❑ Glue
- ❑ Spiral notebook, pages
- ❑ A bag lunch or lunch money. Lunch costs ______. Milk costs ______.

- ❑ Loose-leaf binder with paper
- ❑ Pocket folder
- ❑ Art smock (old T-shirt)
- ❑ Sneakers on gym days
- ❑ Daily snack
- ❑ Other ______________

I welcome communication with parents and guardians. The best way to reach me is

____.

Please be sure your child gets a good night's sleep and eats a hearty breakfast before school. Provide a quiet, well-lit space for homework. And please try to read with your child every day.

Sincerely,

Student Information Form

Child's name ____

Nickname __________________________ Birthday __________________________

Parent/Guardian's name ____

Address ____

Phone (home) __________________ Phone (work) __________________

Parent/Guardian's name ____

Address ____

Phone (home) __________________ Phone (work) __________________

With whom does your child live? ____

Emergency contact __________________________ Phone __________________

Who has permission to pick up your child at school? __________________

____

Siblings/ages ____

Does your child have any medical conditions, allergies or food restrictions? Please describe.

____

____

After school activities and hobbies ____

Are there any situations at home or in the family that may impact your child's behavior or

performance in school? ____

____

Is there anything else you would like to tell me about your child? __________________

____

____

Please be assured that all information will be kept confidential.

Class Rules

Dear Parents/Guardians,

The children and I have created class rules that we have all agreed to follow this year. Please review these rules with your child.

In the Classroom

____

____

____

____

In the Halls

____

____

On the Playground

____

____

On the Bus

____

____

In Case of Fire

____

____

A Call for Volunteers

I welcome your involvement in our classroom activities. If you would like to be called on from time to time to help out, either in the class-room, at home or by donating supplies, please complete the form below. Thank you!

Name _________________________ Child's name _____________________________

Phone _________________________ Best time to reach you _______________

Please check your areas of interest.

❏ Providing food for special events

❏ Providing supplies or paper goods for special events

❏ Helping with activities in the classroom

    ❏ morning   ❏ afternoon

❏ Helping at home (making phone calls, etc.)

❏ Typing student work

❏ Reading aloud to students

❏ Listening to student readers

❏ Chaperoning field trips

❏ Sharing your special talent, hobby or career (crafts, music, science, etc.)

    Please describe. ____

❏ Other ____

____

____

Our Daily Schedule

School starts at _______________

Snack time _______________

Lunch time _______________

Recess _______________

School ends at _______________

Our Weekly Schedule

Music _______________

Art _______________

Phys. Ed. _______________

Library _______________

_________ _______________

Post your schedule so children will know what to expect each day. Draw a clock face next to each item for younger children. This sheet will also come in handy if you and your class are out of the room and you need to be located. Post it near your classroom door.

Attendance/Grade Chart

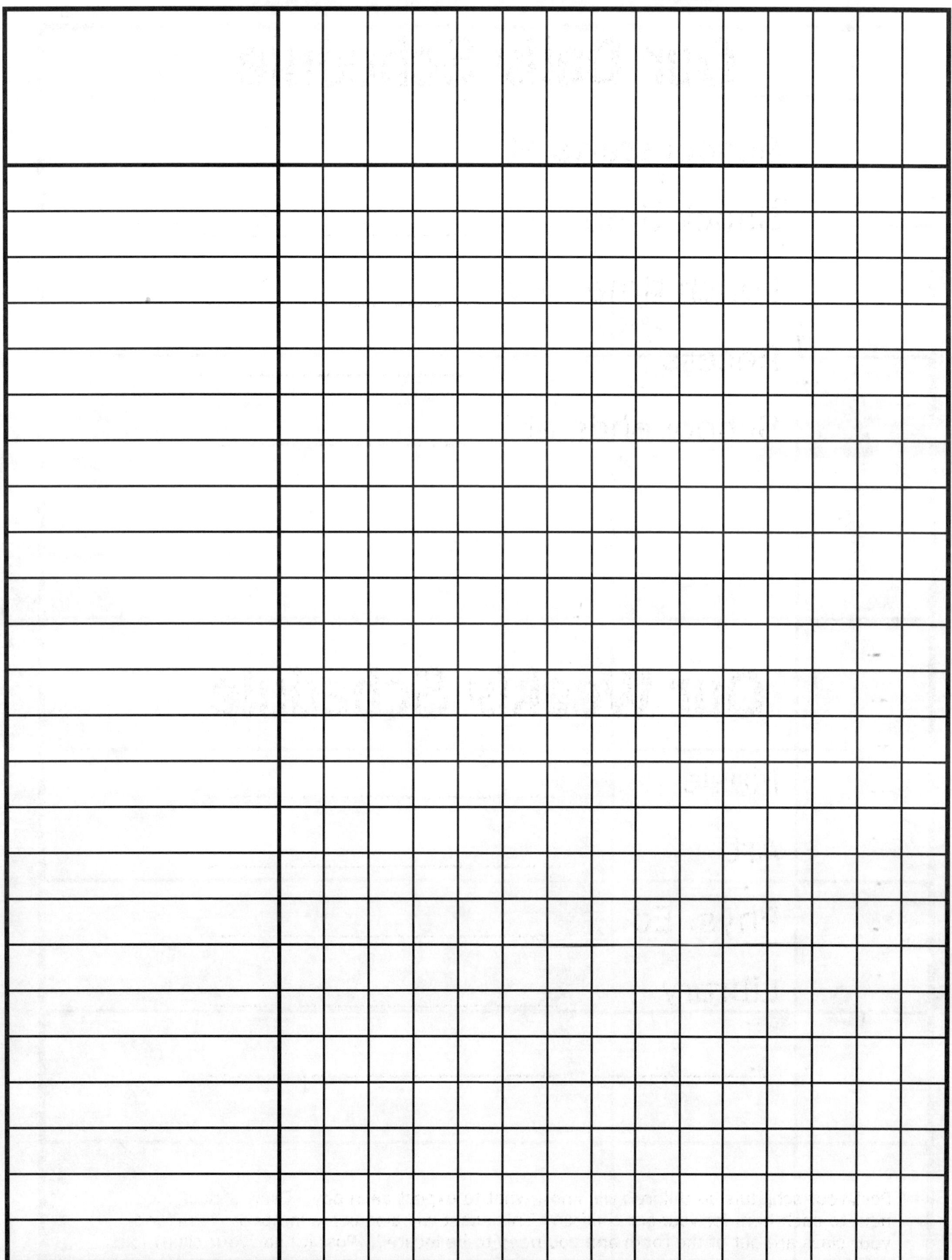

Daily Lesson Plan

Date ________________

Time	Subject	Lesson/Assignment

Today's Homework

Reading Due	**Science** Due
Language Arts/ Due **Spelling**	**Social Studies** Due
	Other Due
Math Due	**Long-Term** Due **Projects**

What's happening in . . .

Sunday	Monday	Tuesday	Wednesday	Thursday	Friday	Saturday

Fill out and send home this versatile calendar to remind families about project due dates,
class trips and activities, school-wide programs, community events and vacation dates.

Date	Teacher	Grade

We're Going on a Field Trip!

Where: ____

When: _____________________ From: _____________________ To: _____________________

Why: ____

What to bring: ____

What to wear: ____

What it costs: _____________________ Transportation: _____________________

- -

Field Trip Permission Slip

Please return this form with field trip payment of _____________________ by _____________________.

____ has my permission to participate in the field

trip to _____________________________________ on _____________________________________.

Parent/Guardian's signature ____

- -

Chaperones are needed for our field trip to _____________________________________

on _____________________. If you are able to join us, please fill out and return this form.

Thank you.

Name_____________________________________ Child's name _____________________________________

Phone _____________________________________ Best time to reach you _____________________

While You Were Out . . .

Name _______________________ Date _______________________

This is the work you missed while you were absent.

Reading
Language Arts/Spelling
Math
Science
Social Studies
Other

Please complete this work by _______________________.

Useful Information for Substitute Teachers

Our Daily Schedule

Snack _______________________

Lunch _______________________

Recess _______________________

Dismissal _______________________

Our Weekly Schedule

Phys. Ed. _______________________

Music _______________________

Art _______________________

Library _______________________

Other _______________________

Teacher to contact if help is needed _______________________ Room __________

Students to call on if help is needed _______________________

Students who leave the room for special classes, medication, etc.

Name _______________ Time _______________ Room _______________

Name _______________ Time _______________ Room _______________

Name _______________ Time _______________ Room _______________

Name _______________ Time _______________ Room _______________

Aides, volunteers, visitors expected _______________________

____

Special duties _______________________

____

Notes _______________________

____

____

____

Testing in Progress

Please do not disturb!

Kid Coupons

Use these coupons to reward good behavior, a job well done or an act of kindness.
Children may redeem coupons for a special treat or privilege.

To __________ Date ______

Because you __________

you may __________

From __________

To __________ Date ______

Because you __________

you may __________

From __________

To __________ Date ______

Because you __________

you may __________

From __________

To __________ Date ______

Because you __________

you may __________

From __________

To __________ Date ______

Because you __________

you may __________

From __________

To __________ Date ______

Because you __________

you may __________

From __________

We Read at My House

Title ____

Author _________________________________ Date _______

I give this book ☆ ☆☆ ☆☆☆ ☆☆☆☆ ☆☆☆☆☆

- -

Title ____

Author _________________________________ Date _______

I give this book ☆ ☆☆ ☆☆☆ ☆☆☆☆ ☆☆☆☆☆

- -

Title ____

Author _________________________________ Date _______

I give this book ☆ ☆☆ ☆☆☆ ☆☆☆☆ ☆☆☆☆☆

- -

Title ____

Author _________________________________ Date _______

I give this book ☆ ☆☆ ☆☆☆ ☆☆☆☆ ☆☆☆☆☆

- -

Title ____

Author _________________________________ Date _______

I give this book ☆ ☆☆ ☆☆☆ ☆☆☆☆ ☆☆☆☆☆

- -

Title ____

Author _________________________________ Date _______

I give this book ☆ ☆☆ ☆☆☆ ☆☆☆☆ ☆☆☆☆☆

- -

New words I have learned _______________________________

____

____

Parent/Guardian's signature _____________________________

Let's Find Out
A Learning Guide for Curious Kids

This is what I already know about ________________________________.

____

____

____

____

____

____

This is what I want to find out about ________________________________.

____

____

____

____

____

____

This is what I have learned about ________________________________.

____

____

____

____

____

A Note from the Teacher

____

____

____

____

____

____

Good News!

____

____

____

____

____

Memo

To:_______________   Date:___________________

From: _______________________________________

Subject: _____________________________________

____

____

____

____

____

Special Announcement!

____

____

____

____

____

____

You're Invited!

Just a Reminder

From the desk of ...

Happy Birthday!

Get Well Soon!

We miss you!

Thank You!

**We really appreciate
your help.**

Theme Units

Room decorations, wall displays, name tags, handouts and lots of little extras all revolving around seven favorite themes let you create a warm, welcoming atmosphere during the first weeks of school and all throughout the year. Browse through this section and then select a theme, or choose a variety of displays and activities from different themes. Discover what inspires you, what meets your curriculum goals and fits your teaching style.

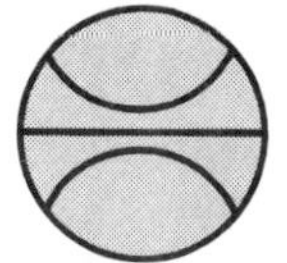

Here are a few tips to help you make the most of the materials in this section:

- Laminate! Your pinups and displays will last for years if you laminate them whenever possible.

- You will want to complete the door decorations, hall signs and some of the bulletin boards and displays before the first day of school. Other projects have been designed to be carried out by the students themselves. These fun activities are great icebreakers for the early part of the school year.

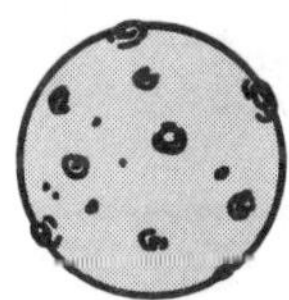

- Check and recheck your student information forms for food allergies before making any of the snacks in this section.

- The web sites included on the books and media pages were up and running at the time of the publication. However, we cannot guarantee that they will still be available when you are ready to access them.

- Each theme includes a post-teaching checklist we call "I Know! I Know!" We know the items on the checklist will not always reflect what you have taught and what your students have learned. Feel free to adapt and modify these pages to encompass the facts and skills you have covered.

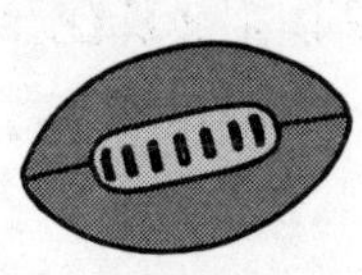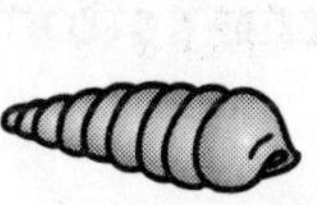

Bugs

A spider weaves her delicate web. A noisy cricket chirps in the grass. An ant drags a crumb five times its size across a picnic blanket. Bugs are everywhere and whether we greet them with an "ugh!" or a smile, kids take to them like bees to a flower. On their knees in the garden, by the edge of a pond or in a dusty corner of the basement, children love to watch and wonder as bugs reveal the secrets of their tiny, busy world.

Just a Note: Although scientists use the word *bugs* to signify only a particular kind of insect, in this unit we use *bugs* loosely to include all insects as well as spiders and centipedes.

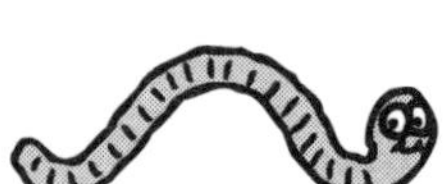

The Hall

This sign, mounted in the hallway, introduces the "buggy" theme and leads the children to your room. Reproducible patterns can be found on pages 51-52. Fill in your name and color the grasshopper. For three-dimensional effects, give the grasshopper plastic googly eyes (available in craft stores), add pipe cleaners for antennae and glue Easter grass along the bottom.

The Door

A decorated door makes each student feel welcome. Copy the patterns on page 53. Color the bees black and yellow. Put your name at the top for a personal touch and write each student's name on a busy bee cut-out.

The Walls

Obedient bugs set a good example for your students. Copy the patterns on pages 49-50 and 54 and add your own class rules.

Follow the Class RULES

1. Listen quietly.
2. Raise your hand.
3. Pay attention.
4. Follow directions.
5. Treat others with respect.

The Walls

Courtesy and safety are priorities on the playground. Write your playground rules on this poster and add the reproducible patterns on pages 55-56.

The Walls

Celebrate one of the rites of childhood with this whimsical bulletin board. Use a dark background and attach the artwork and heading on pages 57-59. Feel free to add plastic googly eyes, pipe cleaners for antennae and other creative touches. Write children's names on tooth cut-outs.

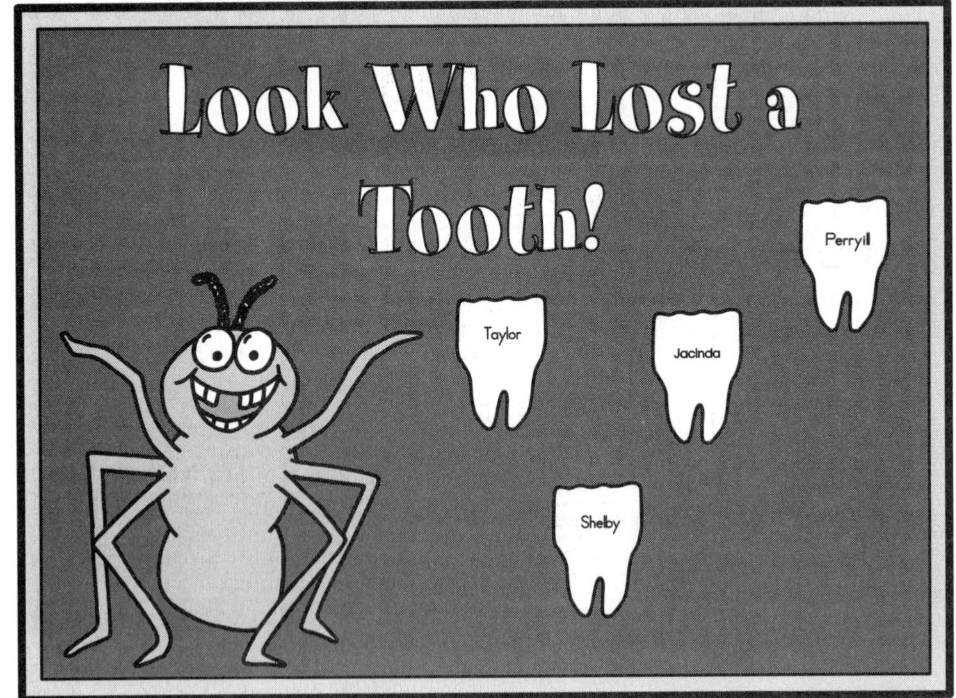

The Walls

Everyone wants a chance to be a "helping hand." Copy art and heading on pages 59-61. As you staple the task cards to the bulletin board, leave an opening at the top. When assigning a task, write a student's name on a slip of paper and tuck it into the opening.

The Walls

Here's a bulletin board for showcasing math wizardry. Reproducible patterns and headings can be found on pages 62-63. Use black pom-poms, sequins or sticker dots for ladybug spots.

The Walls

Highlight special efforts with this dramatic display. Cover your bulletin board with black paper. Copy the heading on page 64 and the moon and the firefly on page 63. Place the heading on top of a sheet of gold foil (available in craft stores) and trace the letters so that they imprint on the foil. Cut out the letters. Cover the lower part of the fireflies with gold foil, as well. Mount everything on the bulletin board, along with students' best work.

The Walls

A web is a favorite graphic organizer. Use this bulletin board to display the spider webs on page 42 or any story web. Cover the board with dark paper. Create spider webs by stapling string to the board or drawing with white chalk. To make spiders, have children glue yarn legs to black pom-poms or paper circles. Add the heading on page 65.

The Desks

_______________'s

Folder

To do:

☐ 1. _______________________

☐ 2. _______________________

☐ 3. _______________________

☐ 4. _______________________

☐ 5. _______________________

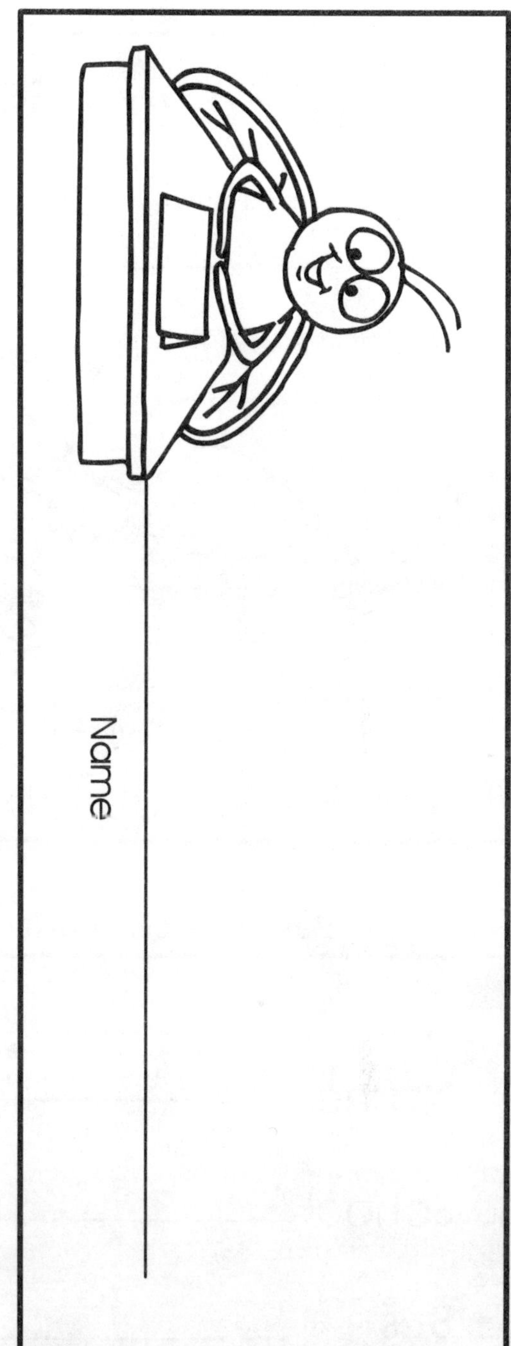

Folder Label: Glue a label on a file folder for each child. Use folders for in-class assignments and homework. Use the checklist to keep track of student work.

Desk Name Tag: Fold a 5½" x 7" (13.95 x 17.78 cm) piece of oaktag in half, lengthwise. Mount name tag on oaktag.

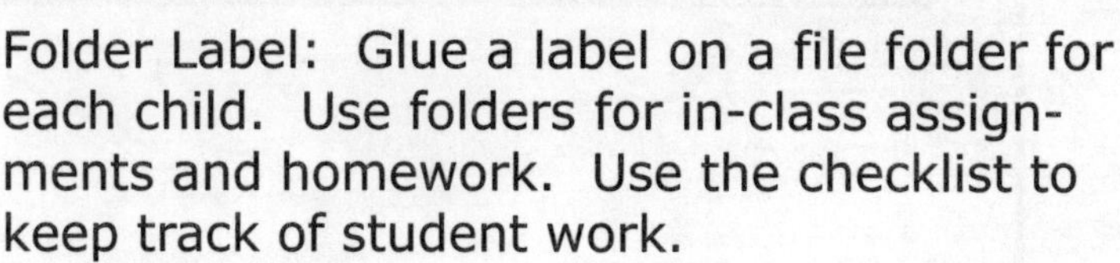

The Children

My name is

____

____

Name

Name _______________________

School _______________________

Bus _______________________

The Awards & Rewards

We count on _________________
for a great job in math!

Signed _________________________

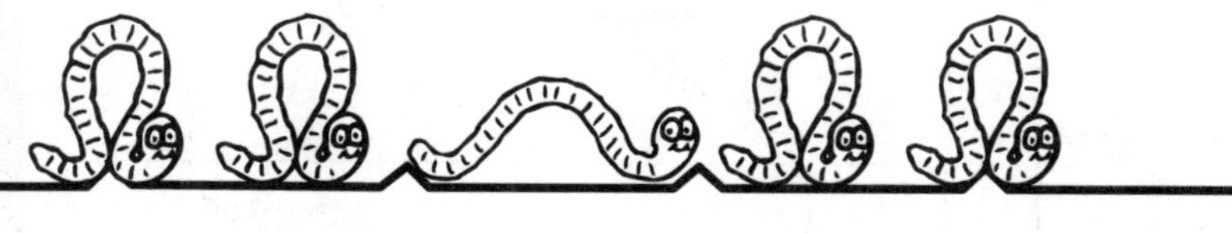

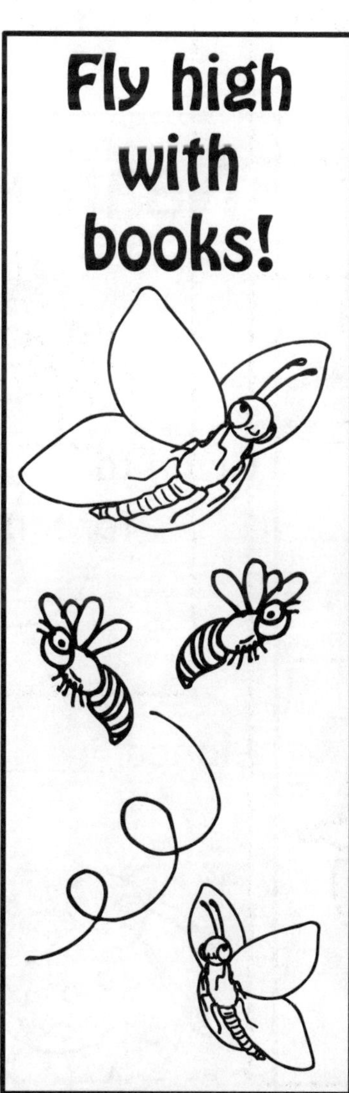

The Awards & Rewards

Outstanding Effort Award

Presented to ________________

By ________________

For ________________

Super Spelling Certificate

Award to ________________

By ________________

For ________________

Neatness Counts Award

Given to ________________
for a nice, neat job!

Signed ________________

I Know! I Know!
All About Bugs

____ I know how many legs and body parts an insect has.

____ I know how many legs and body parts a spider has.

____ I know what metamorphosis is.

____ I know what camouflage is.

____ I know some bugs that are harmful.

____ I know some bugs that are useful.

____ I know where to find bugs in my neighborhood.

Draw some of your favorite bugs below.

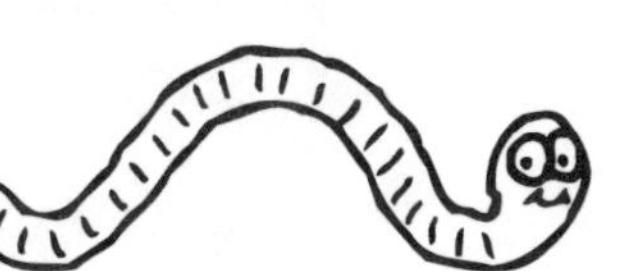

Name _______________________

Eight Facts About Spiders

Spiders are remarkable creatures! Read all about spiders.
Then write a spider fact in each box.

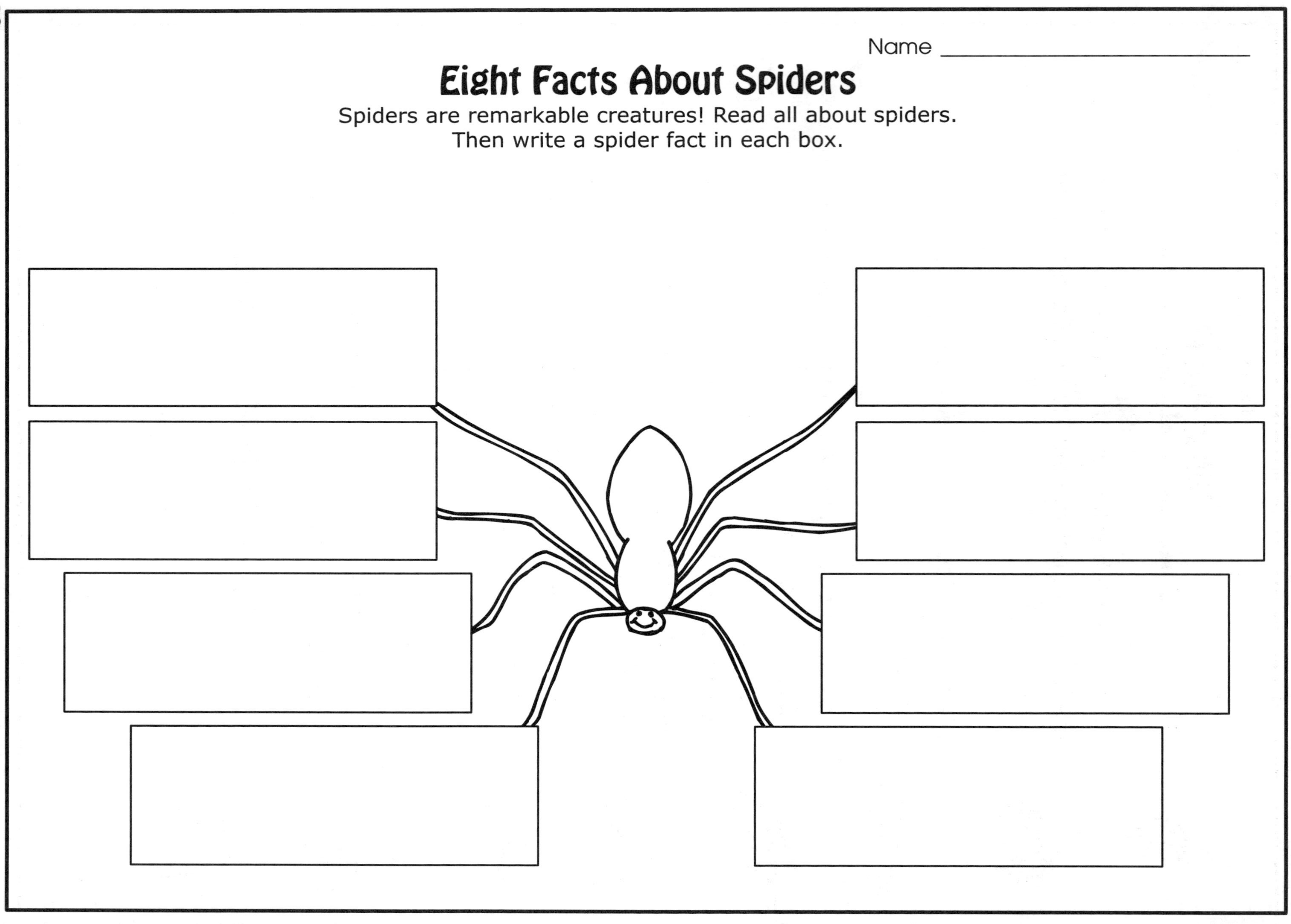

What Am I?

Write the name of each bug in the spaces.

I am red with black spots on my back. Gardeners like
me because I eat the aphids that destroy plants.
I am a _ _ _ _ _ _⃝_.

I have eight legs and I weave a silky web.
I am a _ _⃝_ _ _.

I eat and I eat. I spin a cocoon. Then I turn into a
butterfly! I am a _⃝_ _ _ _ _ _ _ _ _.

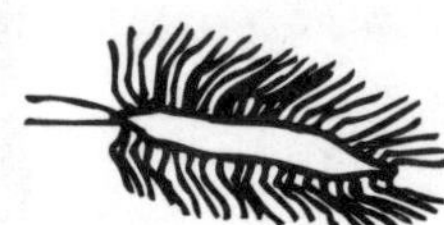

I scurry around gardens and basements and other
dark, wet places. I look like I have one hundred legs.
I am a _ _⃝_ _ _ _ _ _.

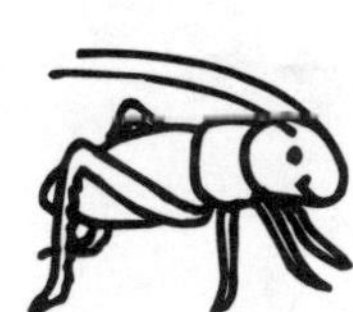

I rub my legs together to make a chirping sound.
I am a _ _ _ _ _ _⃝_.

Now find the answer to this riddle.
Print the circled letters, in order, in the spaces below.

What is the biggest kind of ant?

A _ _ _ _ _!

The Books & Media

Bug Books

What's Inside? Insects
by Angela Royston, Dorling Kindersley, 1992. Peel-back pages reveal fascinating secrets of insects' bodies.

Bright Beetle
by Rich Chrustowski, Henry Holt, 2000. A captivating and factual account of a ladybug's life cycle, with vivid illustrations.

The Grouchy Ladybug
by Eric Carle, HarperCollins, 1996. Using a combination of mosaic illustrations and a story with a moral, this is a great book to introduce a unit on insects.

The New Creepy Crawly Collection
Gareth Stevens, 1996. Discusses bees, beetles, centipedes, dragonflies, snails, spiders, scorpions and worms, each in a separate volume. Descriptive sentences and clear, colorful illustrations.

How Caterpillars Turn into Butterflies
by Jill Bailey, Benchmark Books, 1999. Introduces the metamorphosis of a butterfly.

How Insects Work Together
by Jill Bailey, Benchmark Books, 1999. Examines the lives and survival techniques of social insects—ants, honeybees, termites and wasps—who live together in colonies.

One Hundred Hungry Ants
by Elinor J. Pinczes, Houghton Mifflin, 1999. A whimsical story of 100 very hungry ants in a hurry to get to a picnic. One ant suggests they go in 2 rows of 50 to get there faster; then 4 rows of 25 . . . An enjoyable introduction to division.

The Big Bug Book
by Marjorie Facklam, Little Brown, 1994. Thirteen giant insects are briefly described and dramatically portrayed on two-page spreads with meticulous color illustrations.

Miss Spider's Tea Party
by Donald Kirk, Scholastic, 1994. With splendid poetry and brilliant paintings, this delightful story tells of Miss Spider's attempts to host a tea party only to have the guests decline for fear of being eaten. Follow-ups include *Miss Spider's Wedding*, *Miss Spider's ABC* and *Miss Spider's New Car*.

Videos

A Bug's Life
Disney, 1999. Pixar's irresistible animation and a great story too!

Insects: The Little Things That Run the World
Smithsonian Video, 1989. Explores the wonders of the vast insect world with stunning photography. Takes viewers nose-to-nose with butterflies and inside a beehive.

Web Site

tamu.edu Search "insects in the classroom" for an in-depth site complete with lesson plans for various age groups. Developed by the Department of Entomology at Texas A & M University.

Spider Snacks

Introduce a unit on bugs–or culminate the unit–with these easy-to-make spider cupcakes.

cake mix(es), any flavor
vanilla frosting with green food coloring mixed in
chocolate frosting
black or colored gumdrops (one per student)
mini m&m's® (two per student)
long black licorice strings (one or more per student)
spatulas, dull table knives, scissors, paper plates

- In class, bake cupcakes from a simple box recipe or ask parents to donate plain unfrosted cupcakes, one for each child.
- Set up two bowls of frosting. Have each child frost the top of a cupcake with either frosting, green for grass or chocolate for the body.
- Place a gumdrop in the center of the frosting for soil.

- Place two mini m&m's® (of the same color) in front of the gumdrop for eyes.
- Cut the licorice string into 8 equal parts for legs. (A good lesson in fractions!)
- Bend each licorice leg and attach 4 to each side–spider style–for a creepy, crawly cupcake.

Note: While all-black spiders are common, red spiders exist, too. For a more colorful snack, children may enjoy using colored gumdrops and red licorice legs.

Ants on a Log

Here's a healthy favorite from years gone by.

celery (one stalk per student)
peanut butter or cream cheese with
   cinnamon mixed in
raisins

- Wash and trim celery stalk "logs."
- Spread with peanut butter or cream cheese mixture.
- Sprinkle raisin "ants" on the peanut butter or cream cheese.

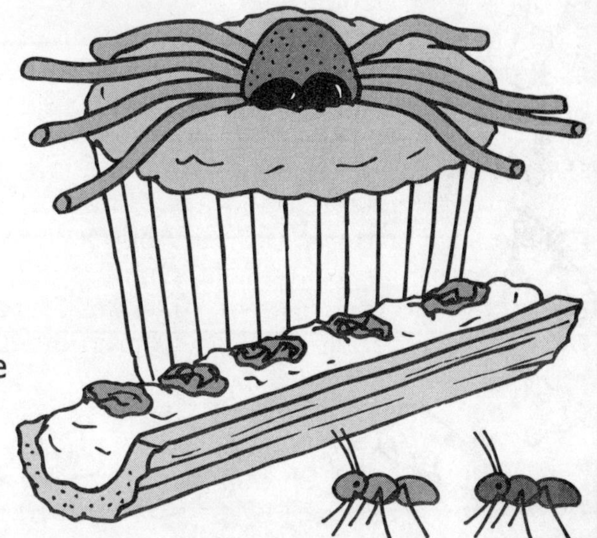

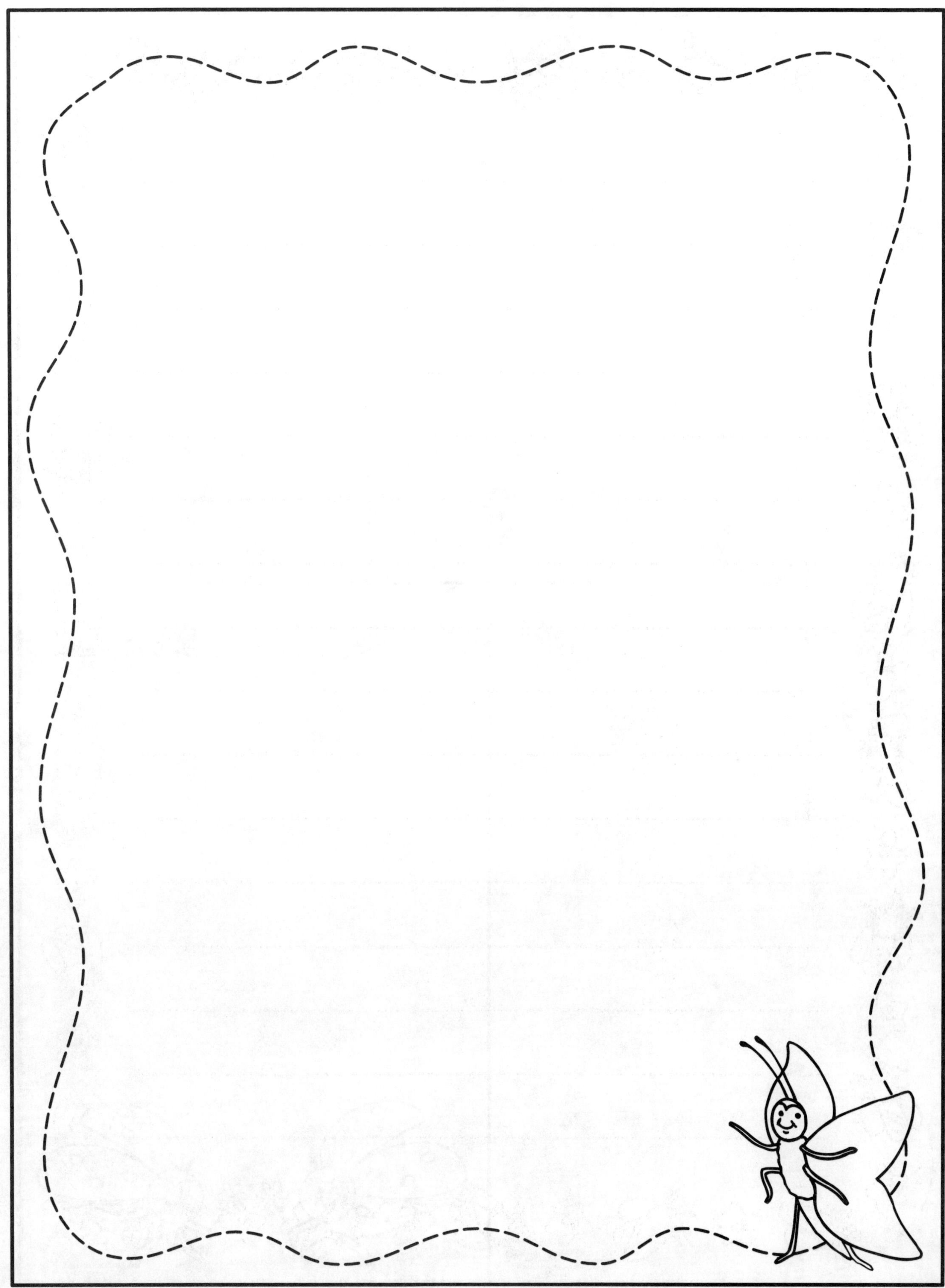

The Clip Art

The Clip Art

Hop this way
to
_______'s
Room

The Reproducibles

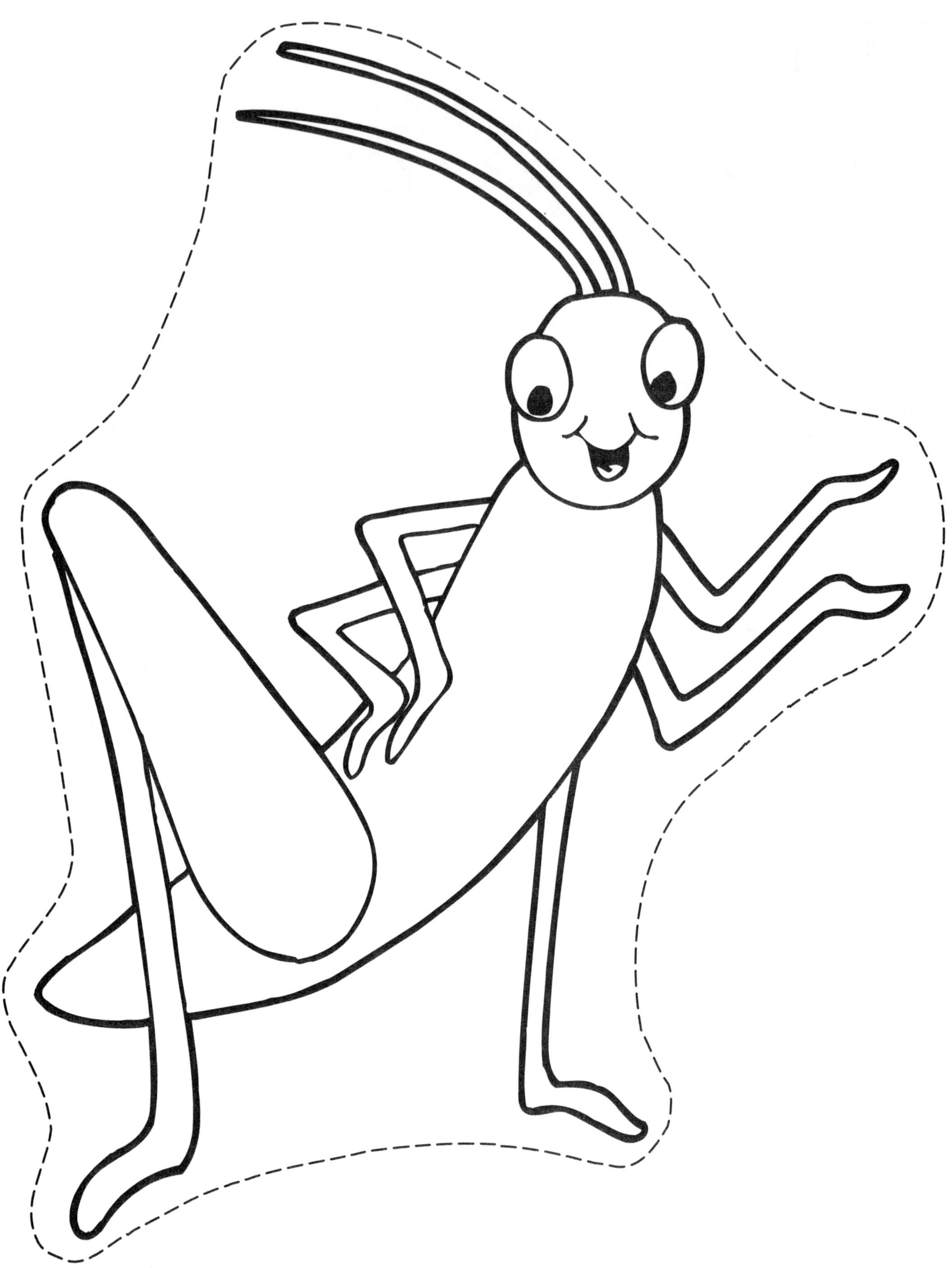

_______________ **'s**

Busy Bees

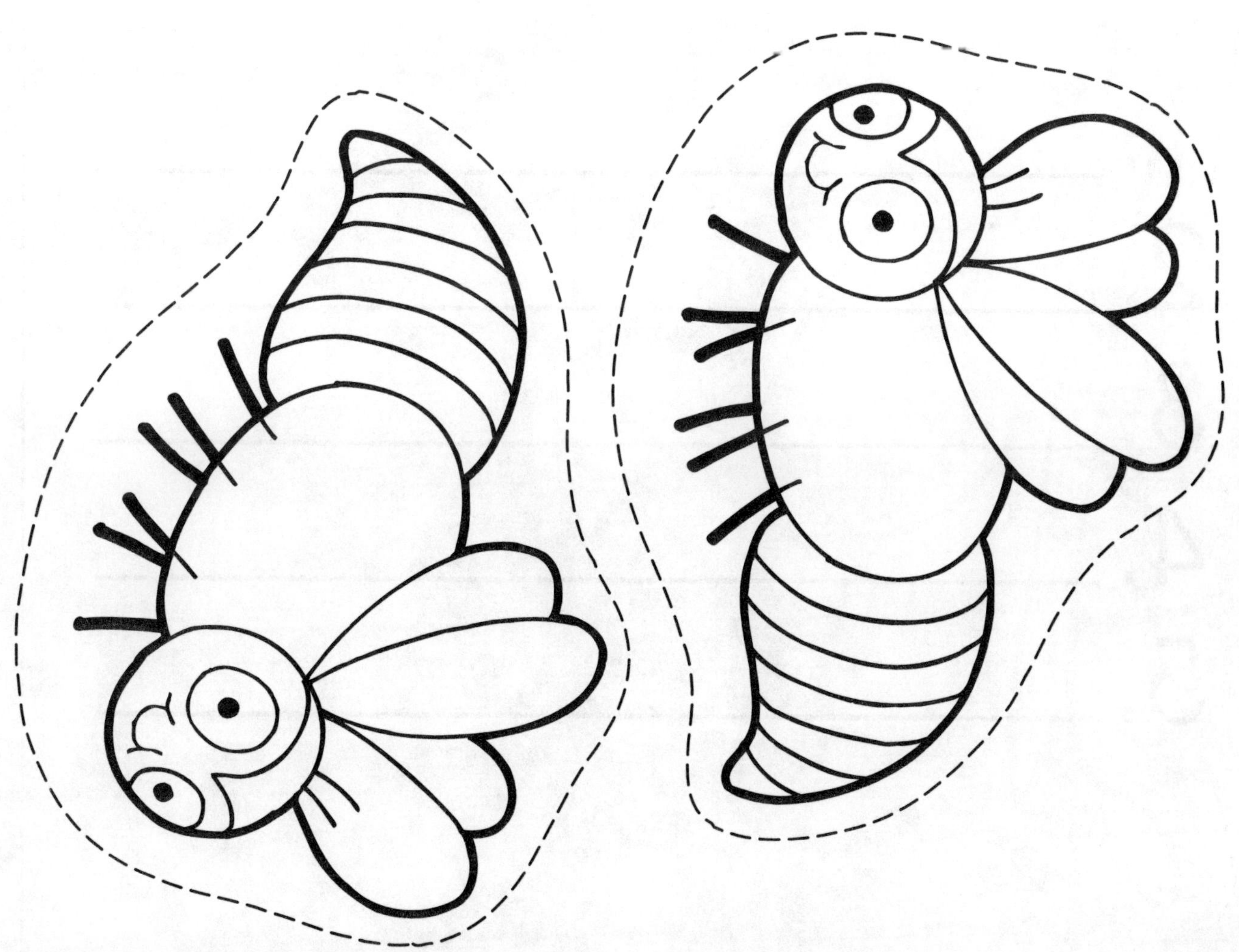

Follow the Class RULES

1. _______________________________

2. _______________________________

3. _______________________________

4. _______________________________

5. _______________________________

Bee Nice on the Playground

The Reproducibles

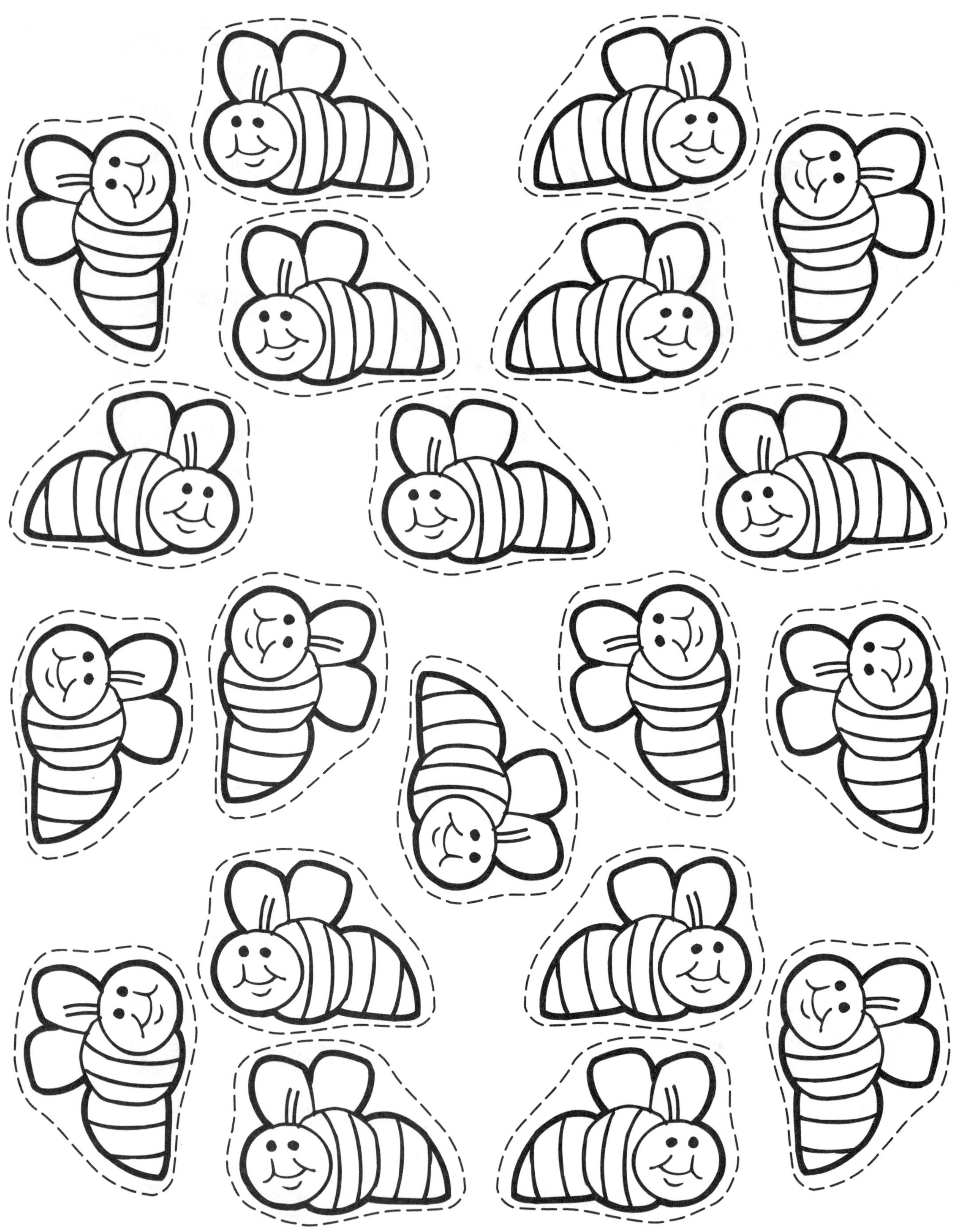

Look Who Lost a Tooth!

The Reproducibles

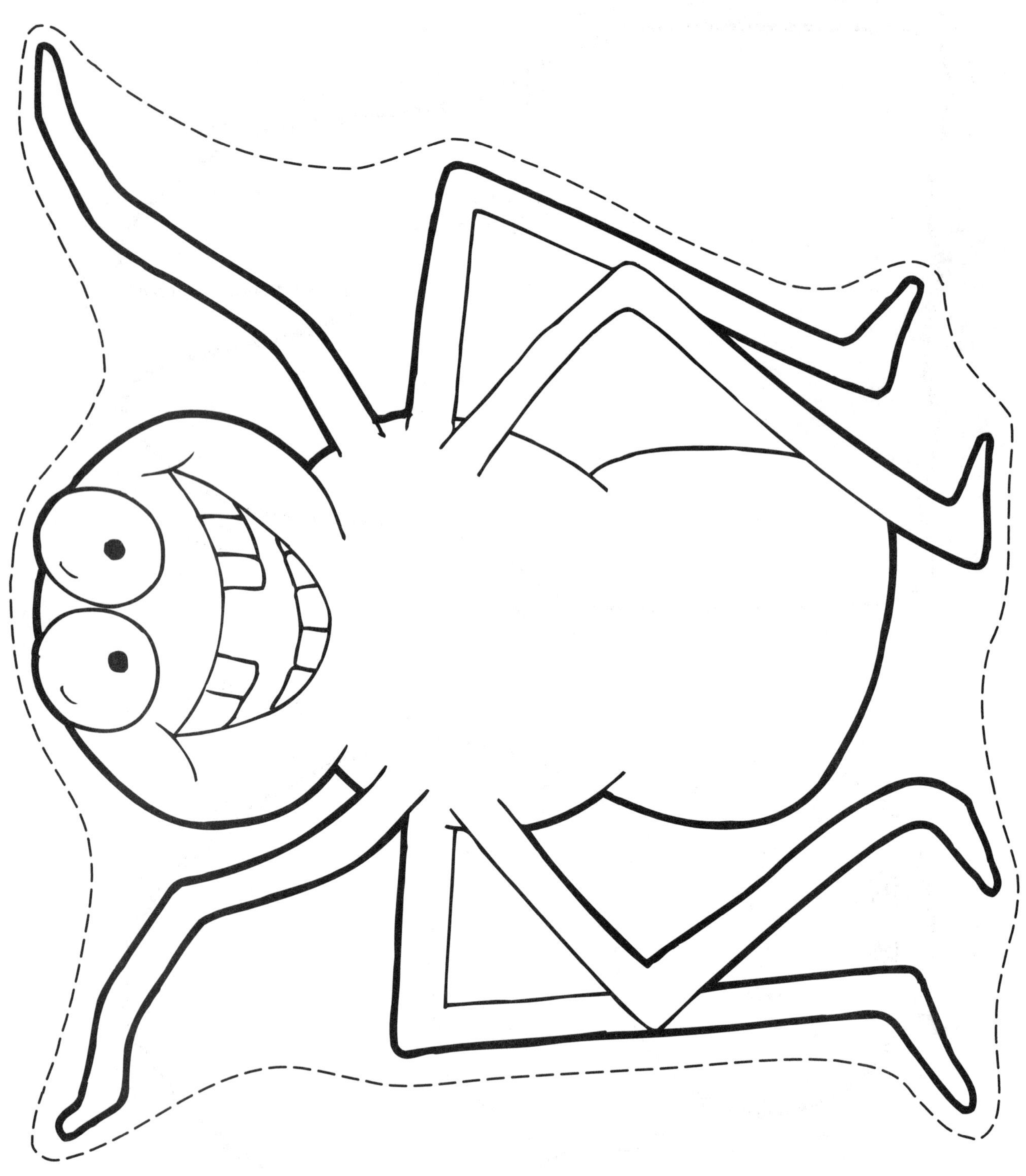

The Reproducibles

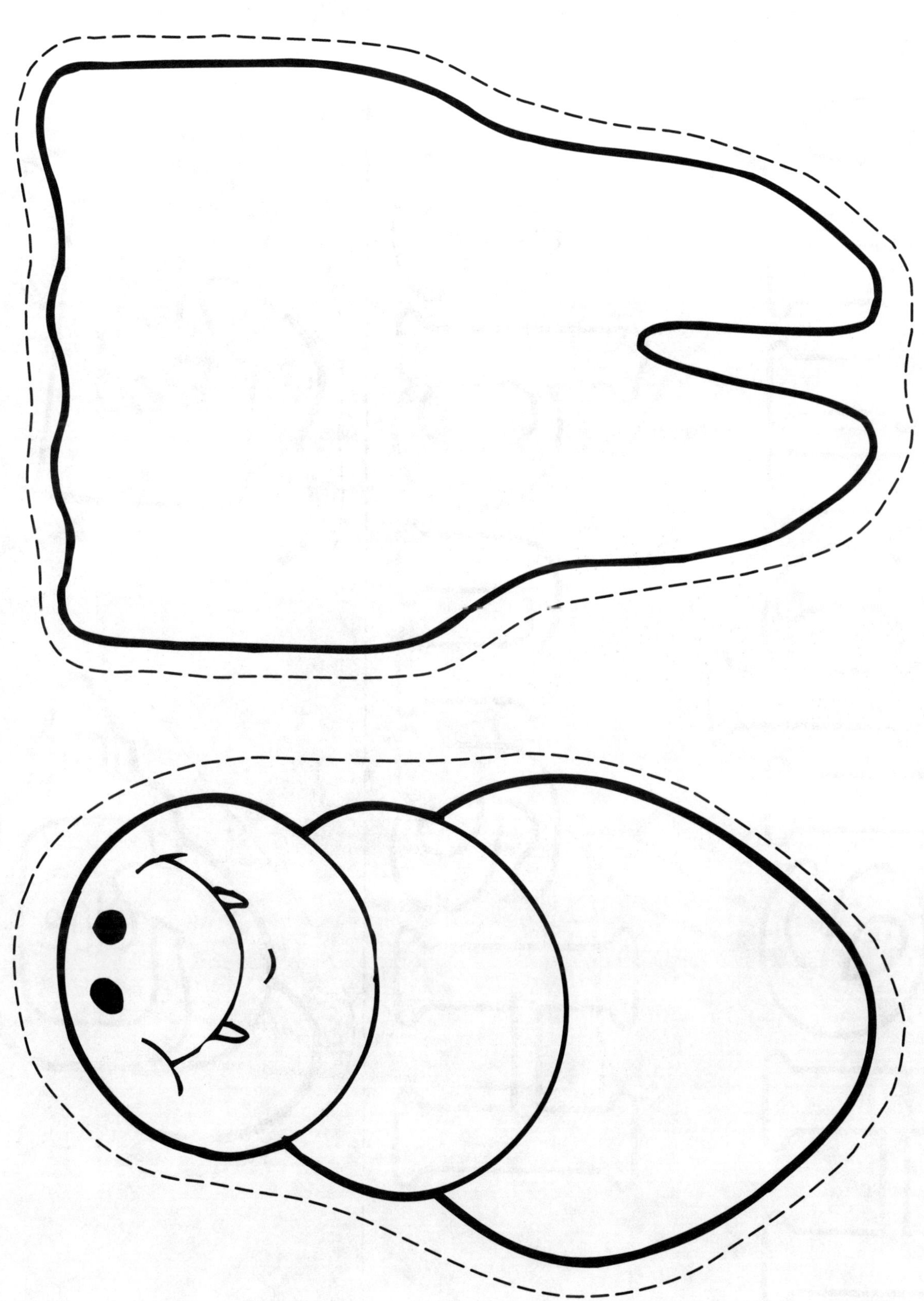

Helping Hands

The Reproducibles

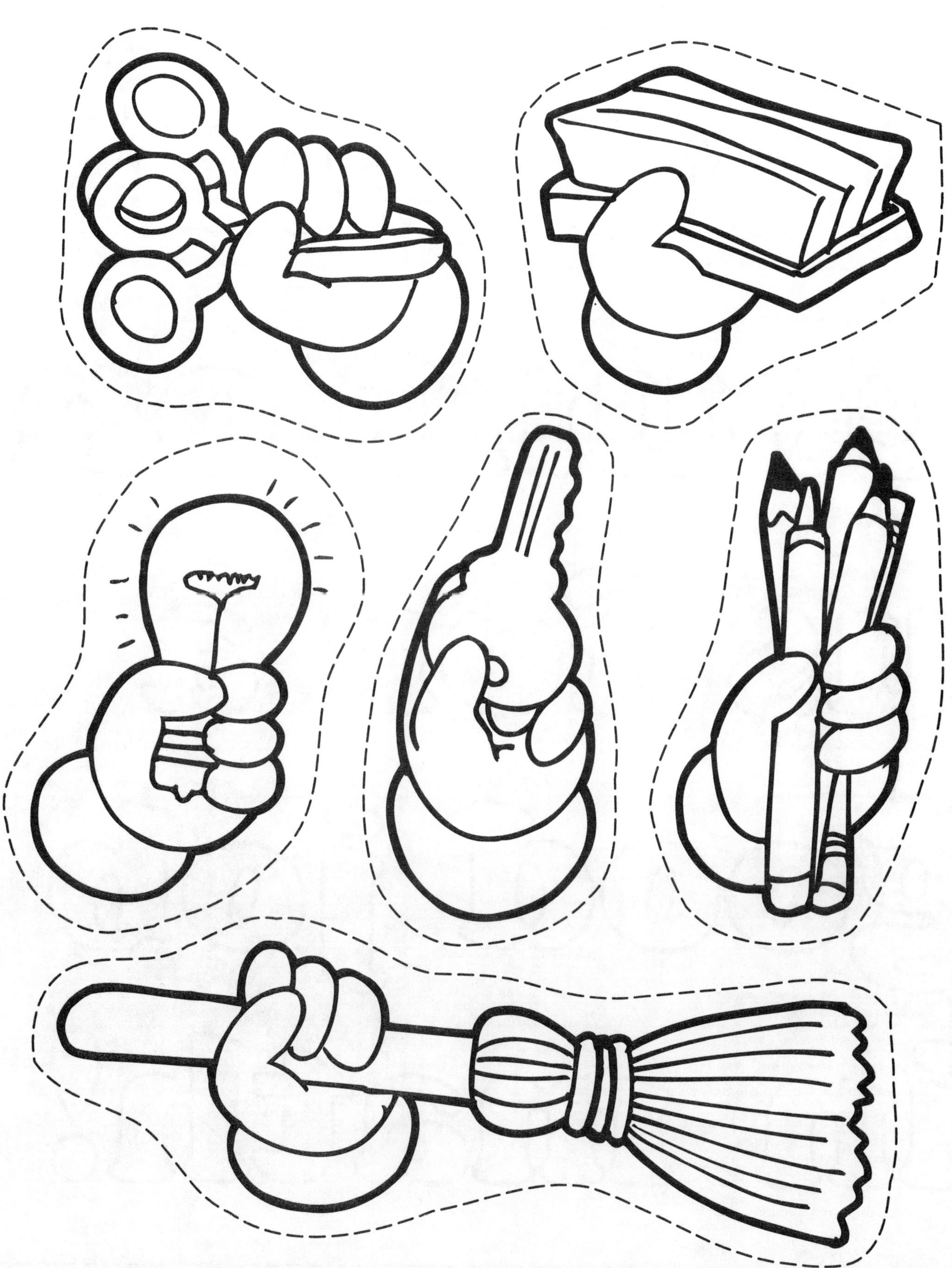

You can count on us for a good job in math!

The Reproducibles

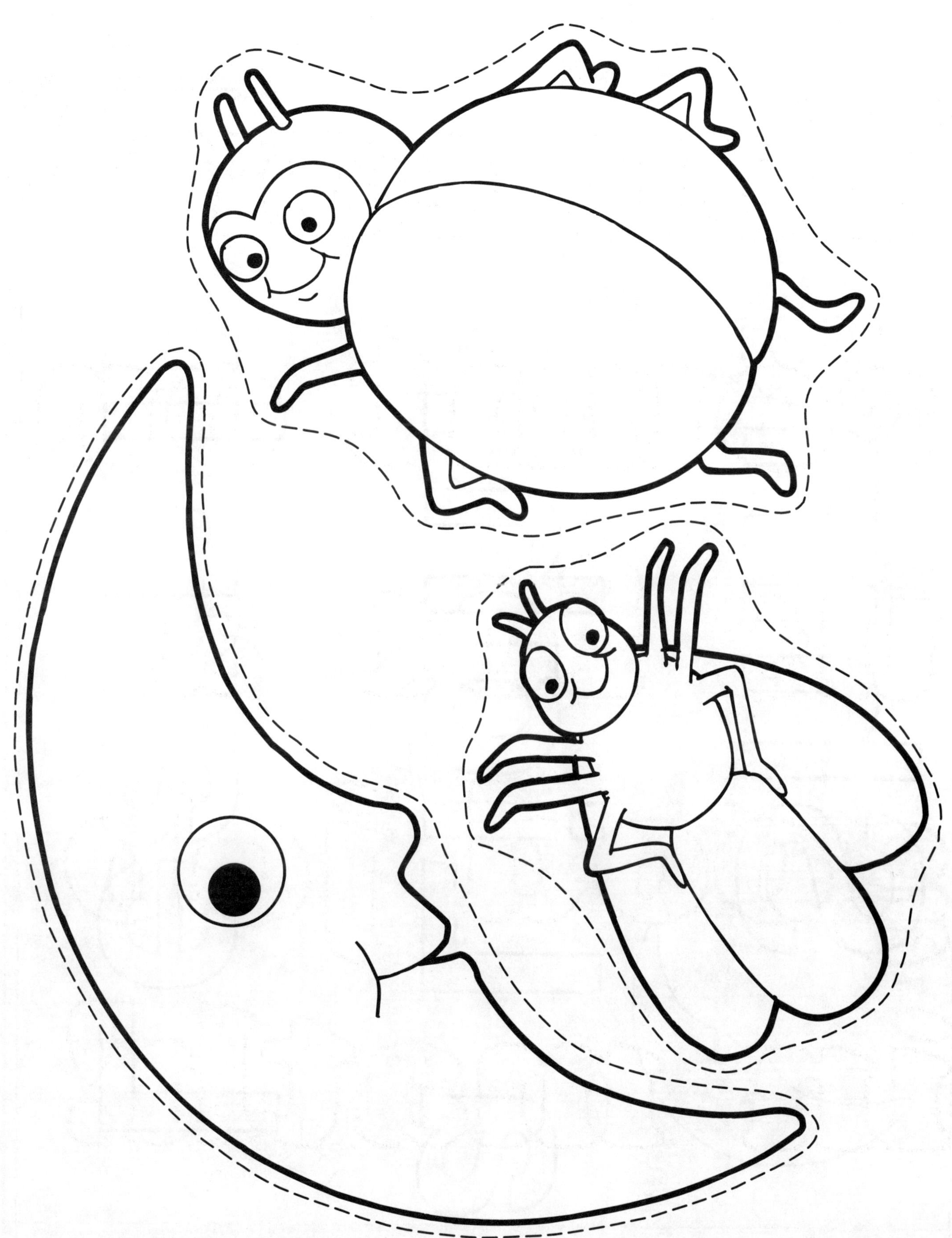

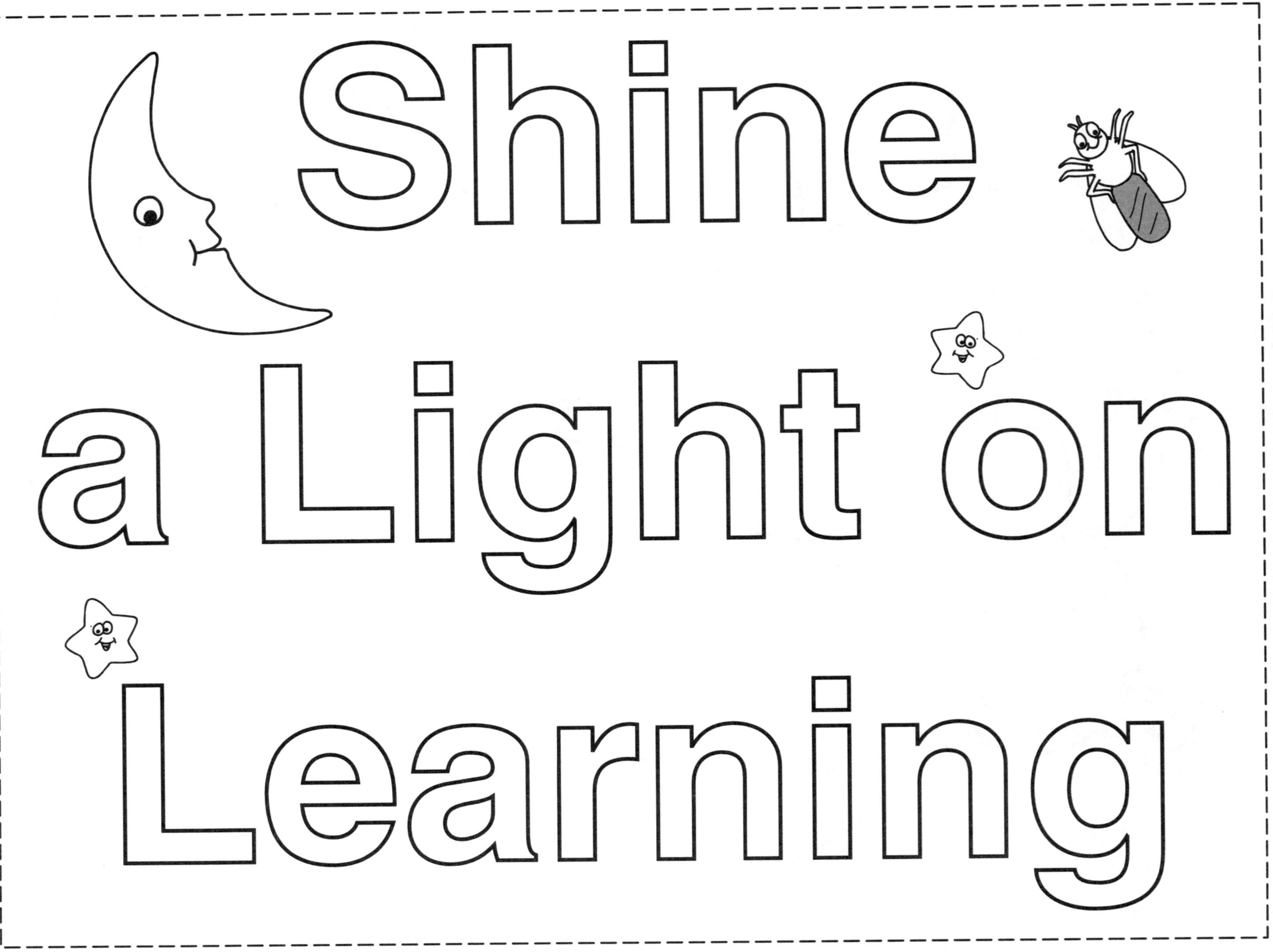
Shine
a Light on
Learning

We Can Weave a Spider Web

Sports

Whether watching a nail-biting finish to the World Series on TV or out on the field booting a soccer ball into a net, kids love sports! Not only are sports fun to watch and even more fun to play, they teach important lessons too–teamwork, perseverance, taking turns, playing by the rules, winning graciously and accepting defeat. The beginning of the school year is a good time to build your own team, a time to encourage cooperation, helpfulness and respect for others, a time to turn a roomful of kids into a community of learners. Team spirit has a place not only on the playing field, but in the classroom as well.

The Hall

On the first day of school, this hallway sign shows children the way to your room and establishes the sports theme. You can make it with the reproducible patterns on pages 84-86.

The Door

Give every member of your team a warm welcome with this spirited door design. Copy the heading on page 84 and fill in your name. Copy the sports symbols on pages 87-89 and add children's names. Create pennants out of colored paper or felt with the patterns on page 86. Later on, ask each child to bring in a small photo to attach to your door display.

Good Sports Play by the Rules

The Walls

A clearly displayed set of class rules reminds your "good sports" to behave appropriately. Reproduce the pattern on page 90 and add your own rules.

The Walls

Give your All-Stars a chance to shine with their own giant sports cards and a spot in the Hall of Fame. You'll find a sports card for children to fill out on page 75. Display finished cards and the headings on page 91 on your bulletin board. Decorate with cut-out or stick-on stars.

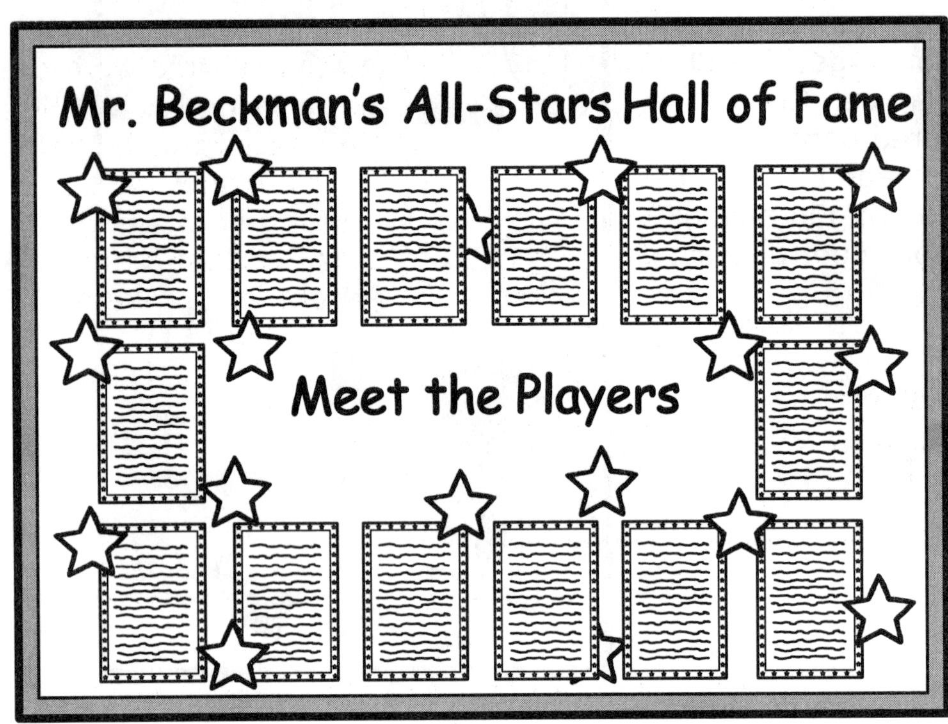

The Walls

Show your young readers you're behind them 100% with a display of their finest book reports, journal reflections or worksheets. You'll find reproducible patterns on pages 92-94. Attach real pom-poms or use the reproducibles from page 94 for extra pizzazz.

The Walls

In math, as in sports, hard work pays off. Create this display of math expertise with the patterns on pages 95-96. Adapt this bulletin board to showcase spelling or language arts by substituting letters for numbers.

The Walls

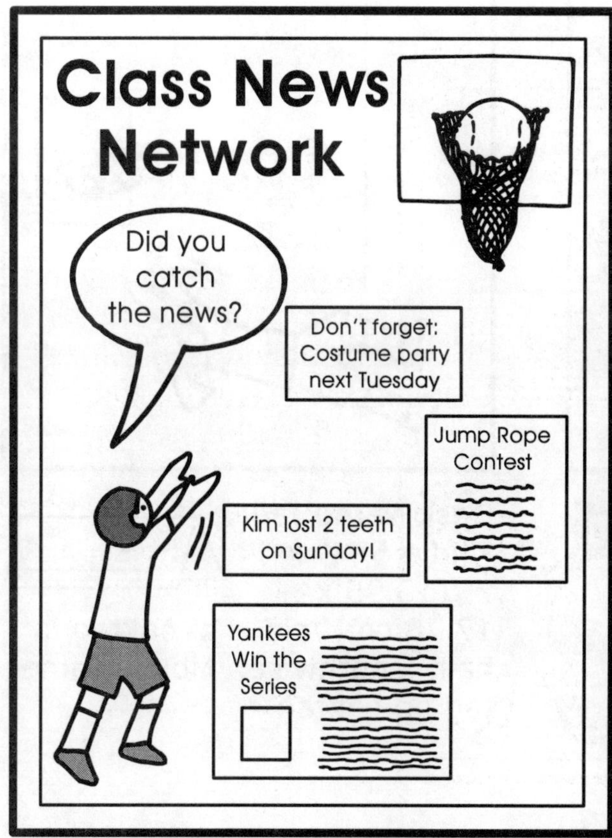

Here's a bulletin board for news and announcements, everything from "Vicky's mom had a baby girl" to "We're going on a field trip next week" to "Freak Snowstorm Hits Hawaii." Copy and attach the heading and illustration on pages 97-98. Create a life-like, 3-D basketball net by stapling a piece of a mesh onion bag to the board. Place a small ball inside the net.

The Desks

_______________'s

Folder

To do:

☐ 1. _______________

☐ 2. _______________

☐ 3. _______________

☐ 4. _______________

☐ 5. _______________

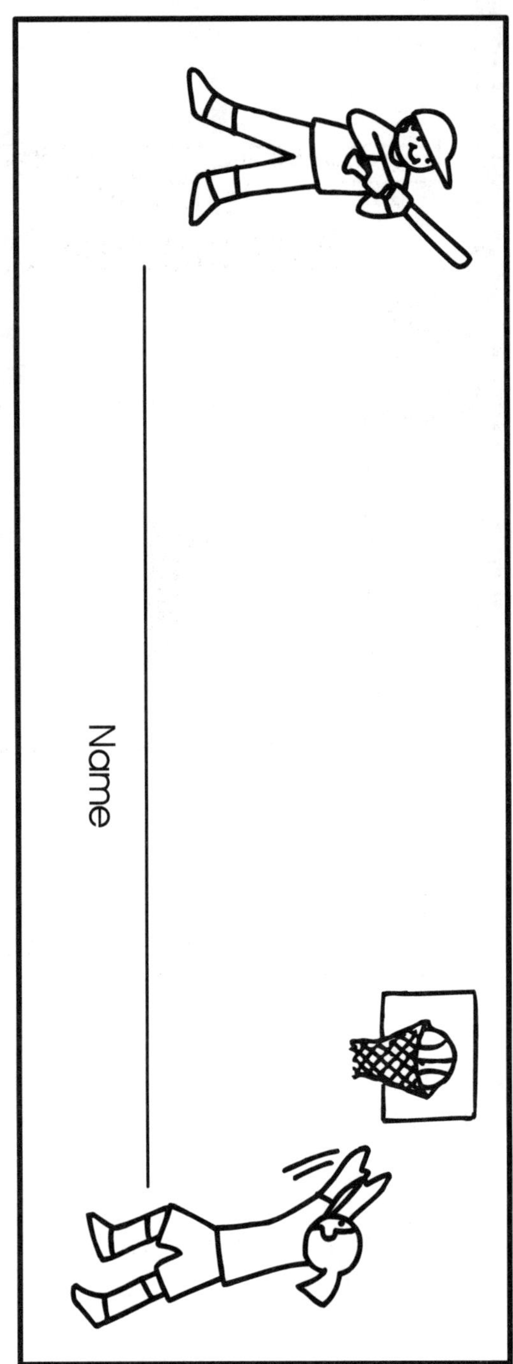

Folder Label: Glue a label on a file folder for each child. Use folders for in-class assignments and homework. Use the checklist to keep track of student work.

Desk Name Tag: Fold a 5$\frac{1}{2}$" x 7" (13.95 x 17.78 cm) piece of oaktag in half, lengthwise. Mount name tag on oaktag.

The Children

My name is

____

1

____
Name

Name _______

School _______

Bus _______

The Awards & Rewards

____

is a Team Player.

Thanks for a great effort!

Presented by ___________________________

For ___________________________

Congratulations!
You've reached your goal!
To
From
For

Hooray!
hit a home run in
today!
From
For

The Hall of Fame
Award
Presented to
By
For

Name _______________________________

I Know! I Know!
All About Sports

_____ I know how to kick a soccer ball.

_____ I know how to throw a football.

_____ I know how to dribble a basketball.

_____ I know how to use a baseball bat safely.

_____ I know my favorite sport. It is _____________________.

_____ I know my favorite team. It is _____________________.

_____ I know my teacher's favorite team. It is _____________.

Draw a picture of yourself and your friends playing a sport below.

My name is ___________________________________.

I am in _______________________ grade.

My birthday is ___________________________.

I am _______________ years old.

I am _______________ inches tall.

The sports I like to play are _______________

___________________________________.

The sports I like to watch are _______________

___________________________________.

My favorite team is _______________________.

My favorite athlete is ______________________.

My favorite sports book or movie is _________

___________________________________.

I like to:

- [ ] run
- [ ] jump
- [ ] throw a ball
- [ ] catch a ball
- [ ] kick a ball
- [ ] dribble a ball
- [ ] shoot baskets
- [ ] ice skate
- [ ] roller skate
- [ ] swim
- [ ] ride a bike
- [ ] dance
- [ ] ski
- [ ] bowl
- [ ] do gymnastics
- [ ] _______________

Put a photo or drawing of yourself here.

What's Your Favorite Sport?

Take a vote for your class's favorite sport. Put one tally mark for each vote next to the sport. Count your tally marks and write in the totals.

Sport	Put tally marks in this column.	Total number of votes
Baseball		
Football		
Soccer		
Hockey		
Basketball		

What is the favorite sport in your class? _______________________________

What is the next favorite sport? _______________________________

What is the least favorite sport? _______________________________

Take another vote. Find out your class's favorite team in each sport.
See who is the class's favorite athlete.

The Books & Media

Sports Books

101 Team Games for Kids by Joe Dinoffer, Coaches Choice, 1999.
Fun, developmentally sound games, drills and exercises, with photographs of each game.

Robert Crowther's Pop-Up Olympics: Amazing Facts and Record Breakers
Candlewick Press, 1996.
Fascinating facts and statistics are brought to life with interactive flaps, wheels and pull-tabs. Swim across a pool, sink baskets in a hoop and straddle the parallel bars while learning about the 1996 Summer Olympic Games.

Olympics! by B.G. Hennessy, Puffin Books, 1996.
A simple overview of the history, preparations, training, and events of the Olympic Games.

The True Book Series, Children's Press.
This series of easy-to-read books with color photos focuses on track and field, figure skating, cycling, swimming and diving, gymnastics and the Summer Olympic Games.

Always Dream by Kristi Yamaguchi, Taylor Publishing, 1998.
The Olympic gold medal ice skater shares her dedication, hard work, pride of heritage and success with young readers.

Changing Kids' Games
by G.S. Don Morris and Jim Stiehl
Human Kinetics Publishing, 1998.
Expertly illustrated, this easy-to-follow book helps you select, plan and evaluate movement games to fit your values, teaching style and the abilities of your students.

Children's Games from Around the World
by Glenn Kirchner, Allyn & Bacon, 2000.
In this collection of games from 50 countries, the author focuses on the universality of traditional favorites. An excellent teacher resource.

Bat, Ball, Glove by William Jaspersohn, Little, Brown & Company, 1989.
Describes how and where baseball equipment is manufactured. Beginning-to-end photographs make this an informative and unusual sports book.

Meet the Women of American Soccer: An Inside Look at America's Team
by Wayne Coffey, Scholastic, 1999.
A scrapbook of color photos relates the trials, training and personal stories of the 1999 World Cup Team members.

Books by **Matt Christopher**
Don't miss the stories of one of the most prolific sports writers for kids. His fiction and nonfiction titles range from ***Great Moments in Football History*** to ***Baseball Jokes and Riddles*** to ***On the Ice with Wayne Gretzky.***

The Easy Hockey Book by Jonah Kalb, Houghton Mifflin, 1977.
An introduction for hockey beginners includes how to pass, stickhandle, skate, shoot, obtain equipment and sharpen skates.

Sports! Sports! Sports! A Poetry Collection
by Lee Bennett Hopkins, HarperCollins, 2000.
A collection of 20 short, cheery poems celebrate the joys and frustrations of children's favorite sports.

A Very Young Gymnast by Jill Krementz, Knopf, 1976.
A renowned photographer follows a real little girl as she trains for and attends an international gymnastics demonstration. Enjoy the stories of a very young rider, skier and skater in the other books in this well-loved series.

Magazines

Family Fun, September, 1999.
Games That Teach Sports
Many suggestions for simple games designed to teach kids the basics of team sports using fewer players, basic equipment and less space.

Sports Illustrated for Kids entices even the most reluctant readers with articles about sports heroes, young athletes, sports skills and puzzles and games.

Software

The Backyard Sports Series
Humongous Entertainment.
Entertaining sports simulation games starring teams of neighborhood kids, boys and girls, culturally diverse and differently abled. Includes Backyard Soccer, Backyard Baseball, Backyard Football.

Ballpark Favorite

Ask parents to donate hot dogs, rolls, mustard, ketchup, popcorn, frozen treats and juice or soft drinks. If possible, have parents cook hot dogs at home and seal them tightly in aluminum foil. If brought into school within an hour of cooking, the hot dogs will stay hot. Serve this popular baseball treat in class, on the playground or in a nearby park. Invite children to bring in baseball caps and play a few innings. This is a great activity to tie in with the October World Series games.

Olympic Medals

Your wonderful class deserves a medal! Celebrate special effort, good sportsmanship and teamwork with this delicious treat.

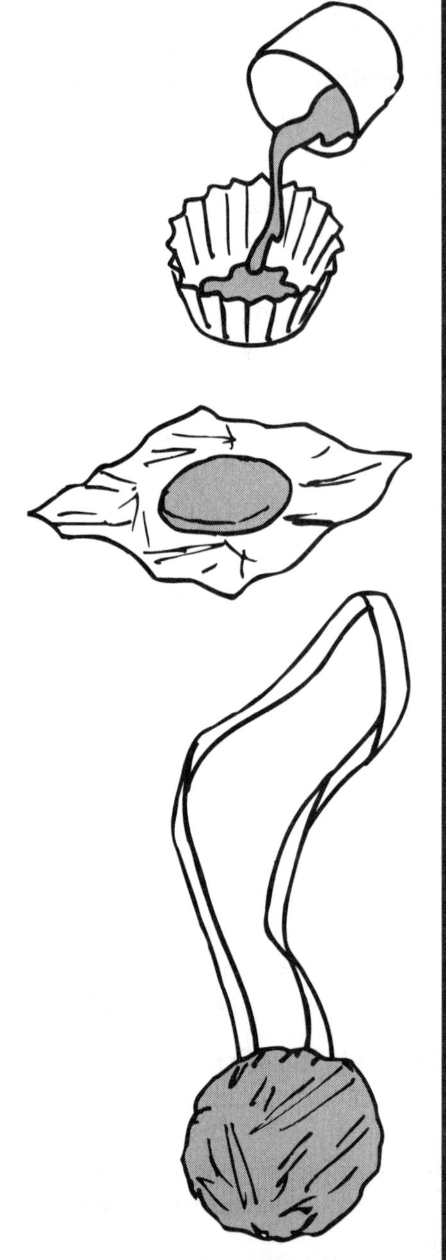

1/2 oz. of chocolate per student
paper cupcake liners
baking sheet
aluminum foil
3 feet (1 m) of ribbon or yarn per student

- Have an adult melt chocolate in the top of a double boiler.

- Place cupcake liners on a baking sheet.

- Pour a thin layer of melted chocolate into each liner. Let chocolate cool and set.

- When set, gently push chocolate disks out of liners.

- Wrap each one neatly in a piece of aluminum foil.

- Tape ribbon or yarn to the back of each aluminum-covered chocolate "medal."

- Wear, eat, enjoy!

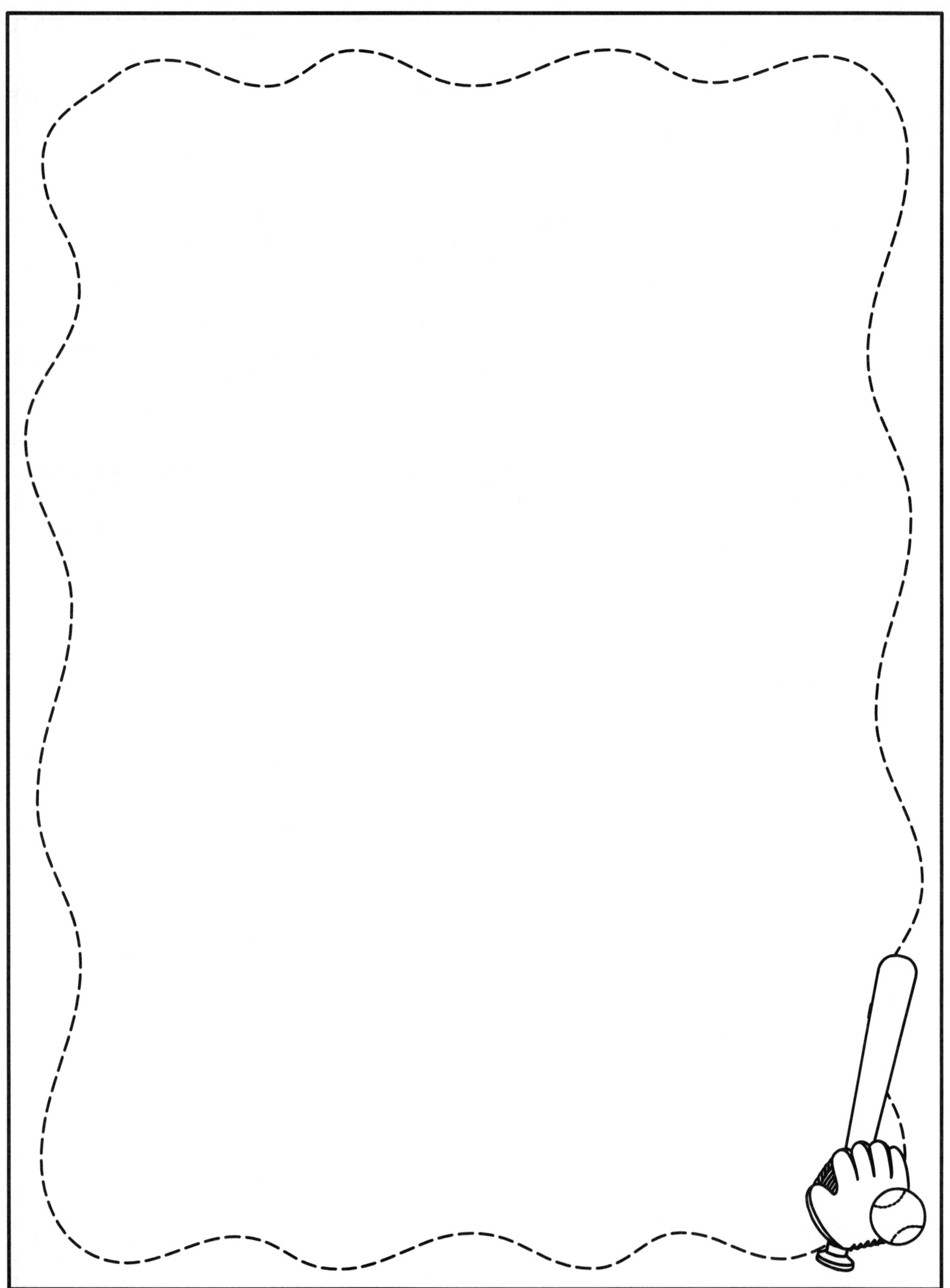

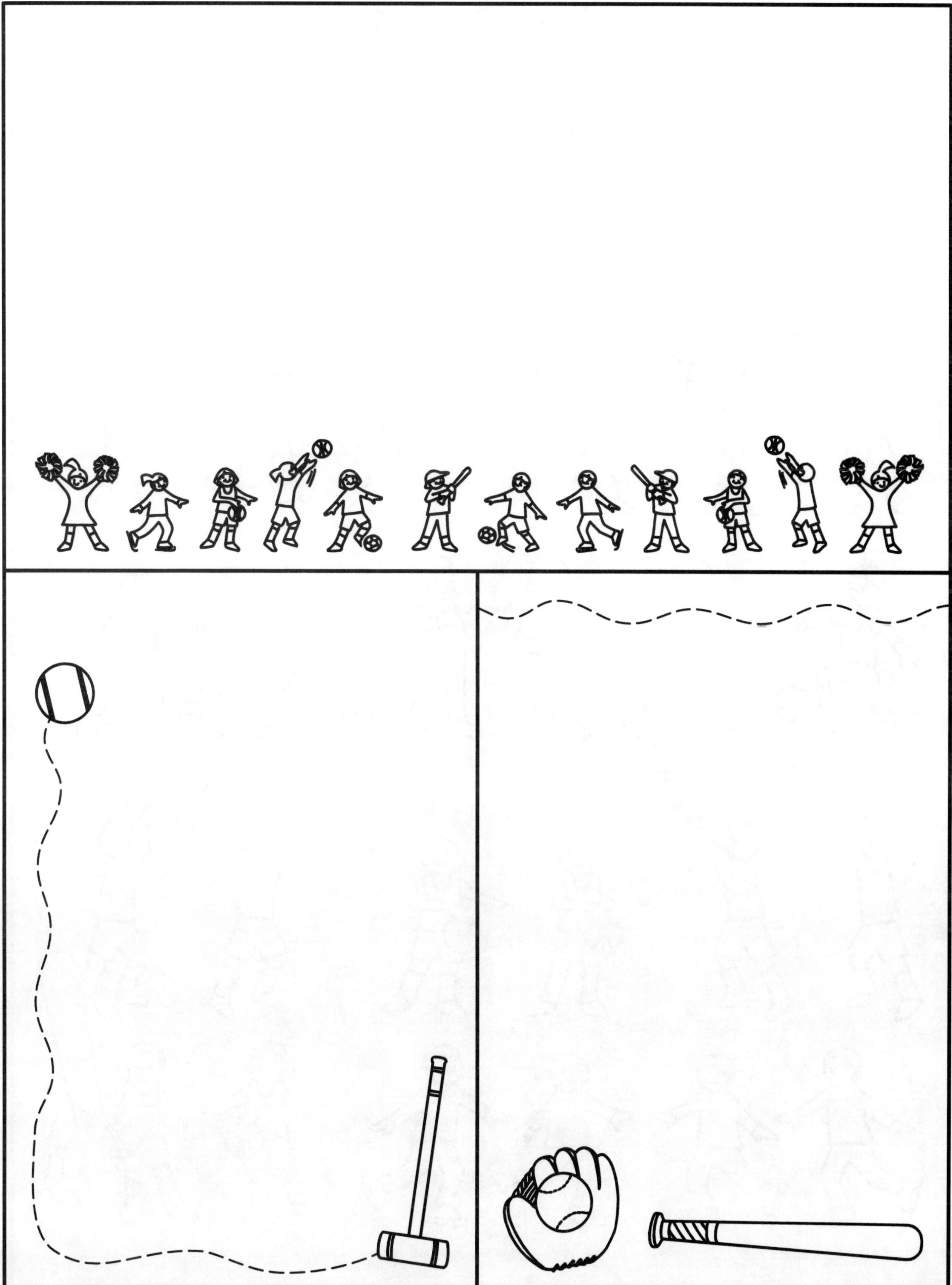

The Clip Art

The Clip Art

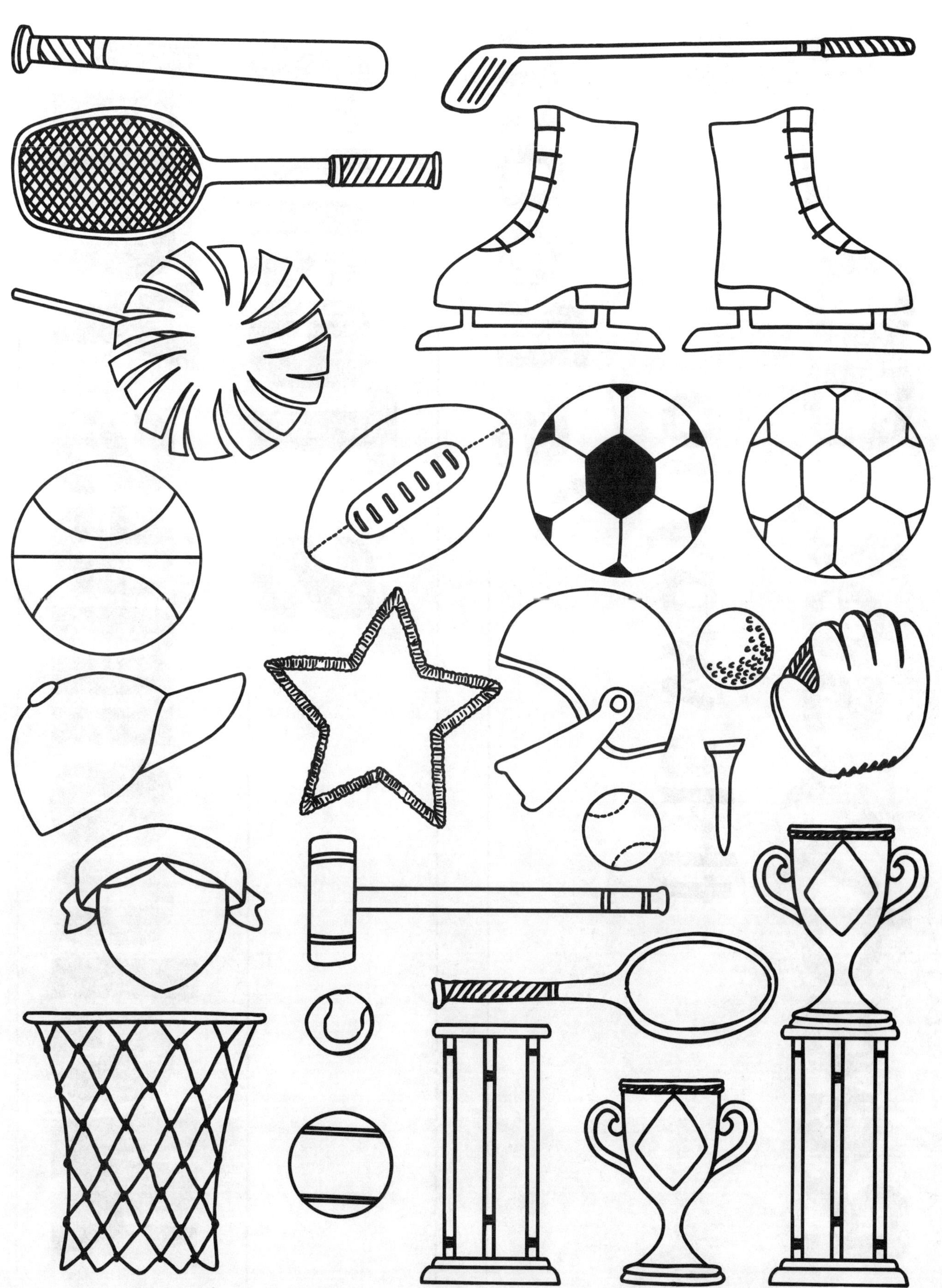

Ready, set, GO . . .

this way to

______________'s Room

______________'s Team

Welcomes You!

The Reproducibles

Rah
#1
#1
Go! Go! Go!
Go Team

The Reproducibles

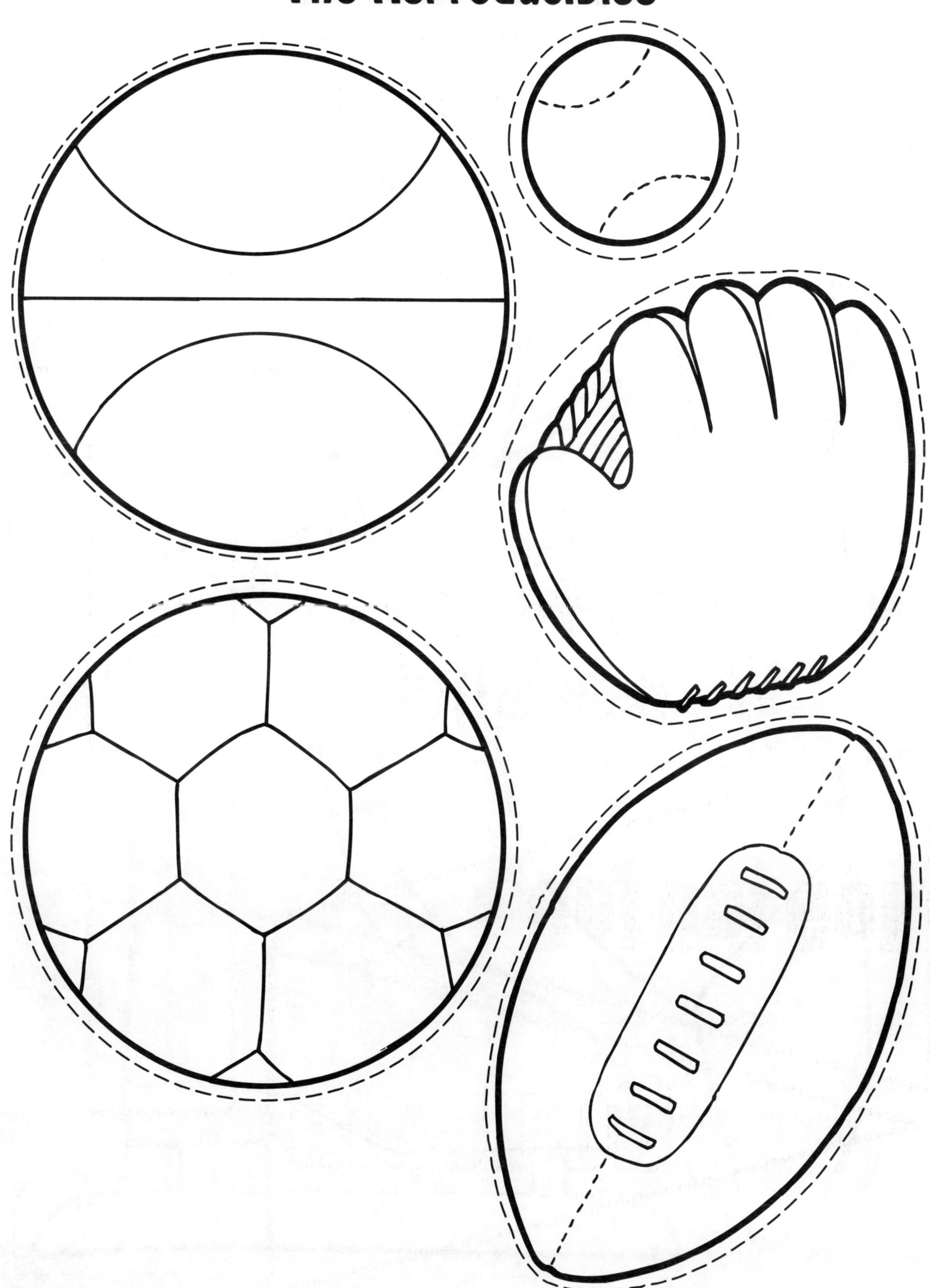

The Reproducibles

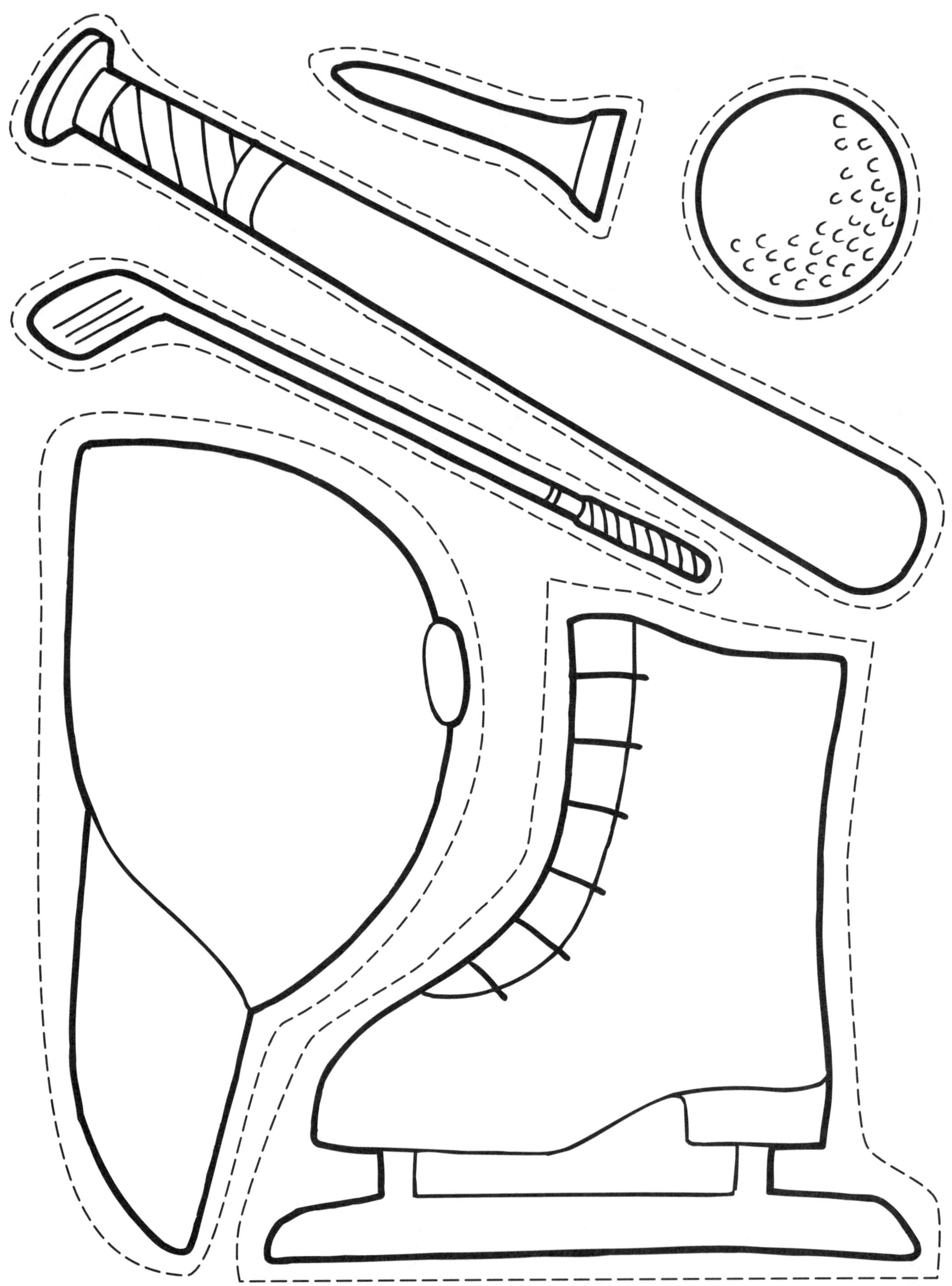

The Reproducibles

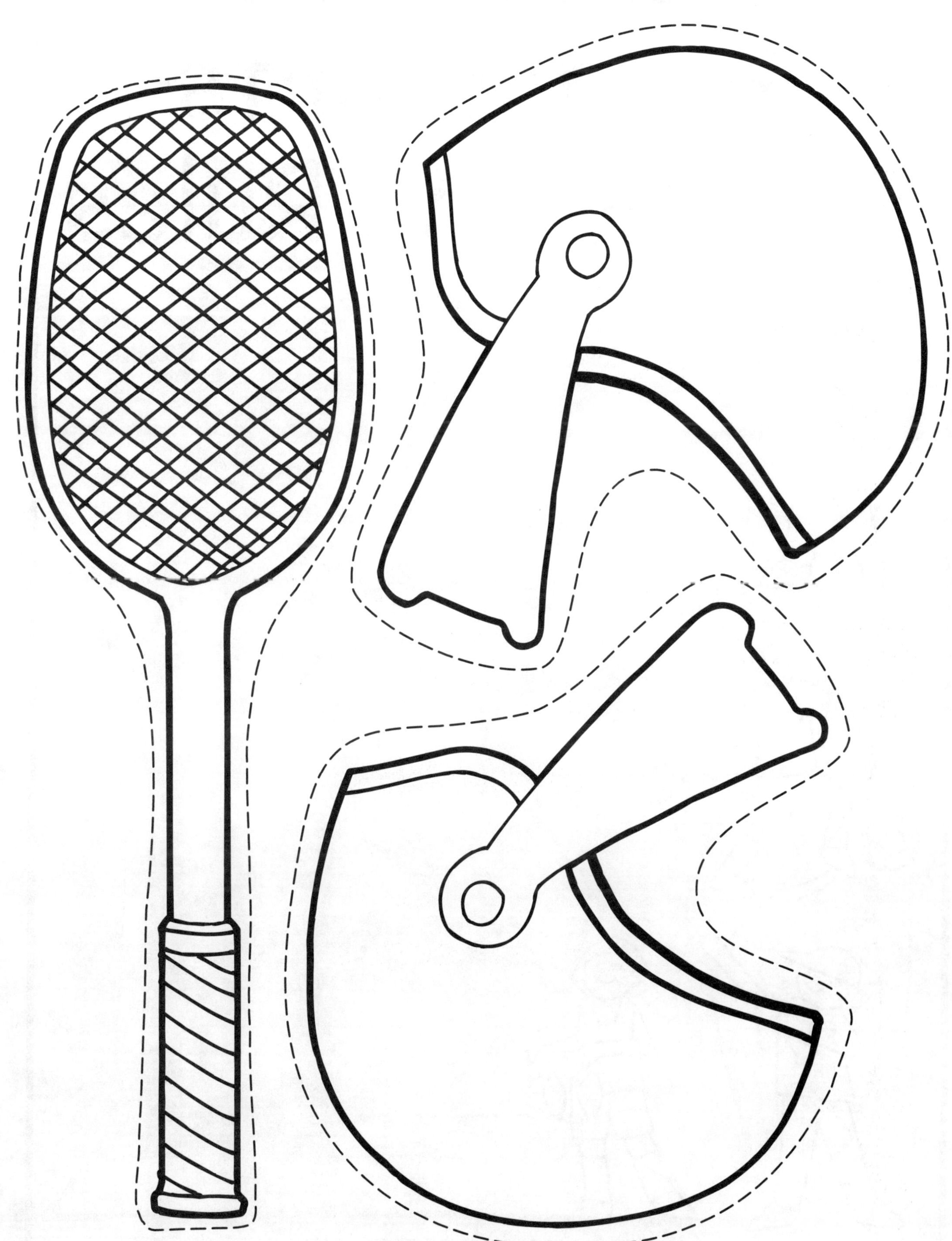

Good Sports
Play by the Rules

All-Stars

Hall of

Fame

's

Meet the

Players

Three Cheers

for Reading!

It's exercise

for your brain.

The Reproducibles

The Reproducibles

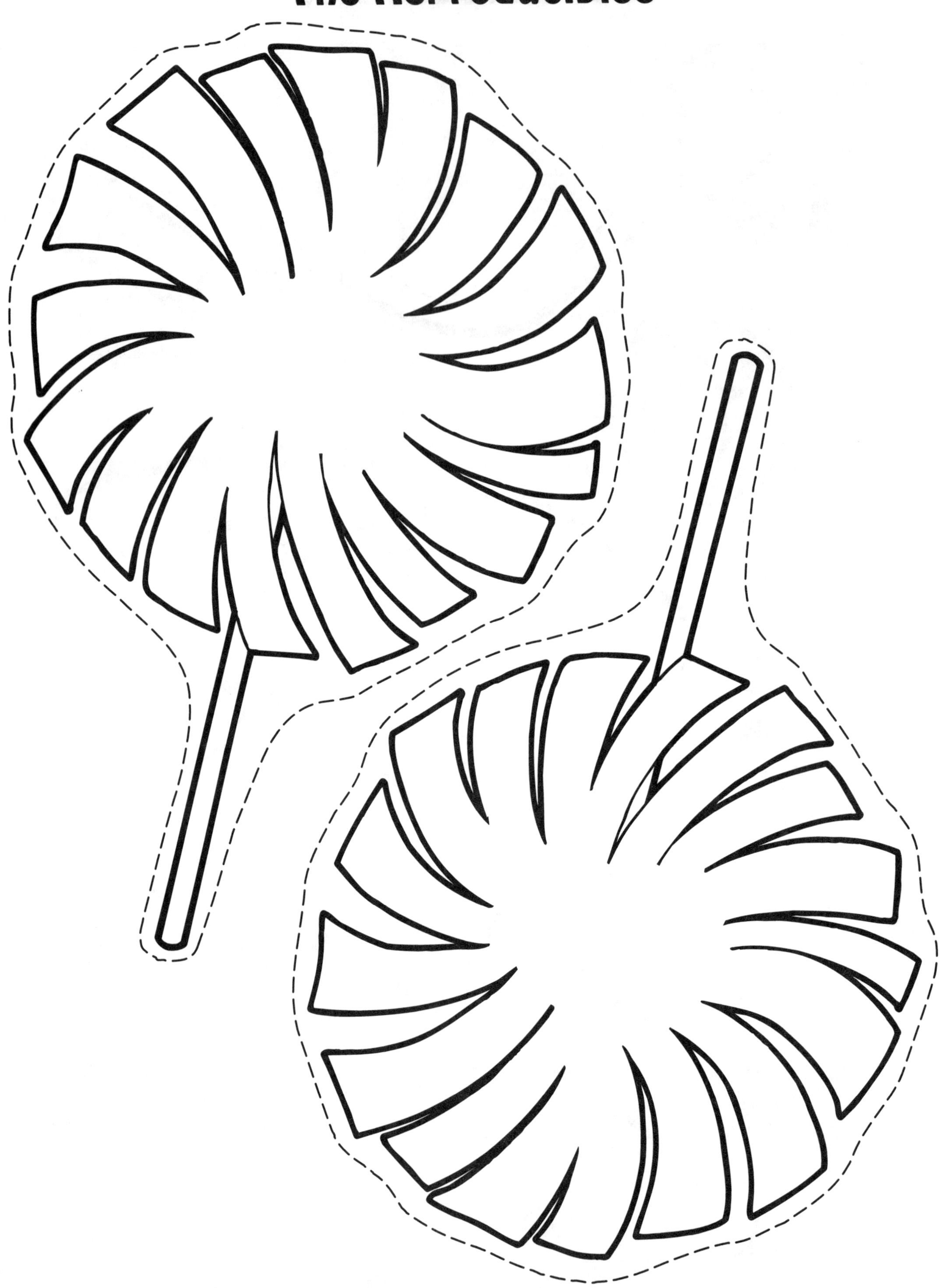

We get a kick
out of MATH!

12
3
5
4

The Reproducibles

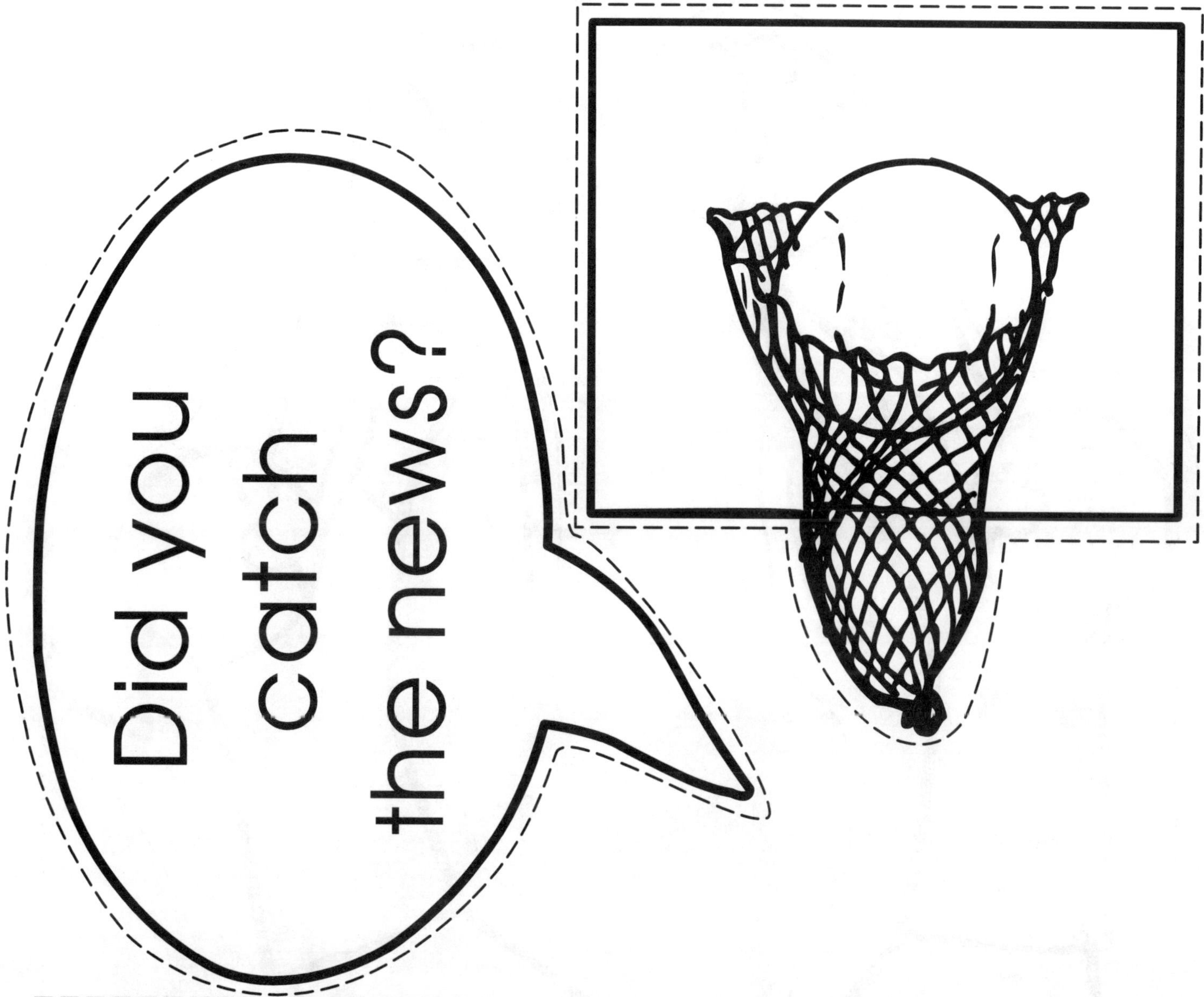

Class News Network

The Reproducibles

Rain Forest

From the damp, dark forest floor, crawling with insects, snakes and rodents, to the sun-filled treetops where monkeys and birds swoop among the branches, tropical rain forests teem with life. Although the statistics astonish us–the rain forest is home to 70% of the world's 10 million plant and animal species–they disturb us as well. According to scientists, nearly half of the rain forests on Earth have already been destroyed by humans, and the rest are rapidly disappearing. Enlightening children, the next generation, to the abundant diversity of life in the rain forest, to the beauty and value of this precious, fragile resource, means hope for its survival.

The Door

Lush, tropical greenery sets the stage for a classroom rain forest adventure. Cut tree trunks out of crumpled brown butcher paper. Use crumpled green tissue paper for leaves and brown and green yarn for vines. Copy the heading on page 119 and the reproducibles on pages 120-122 onto bright Day-Glo™ paper. Write children's names on the creatures. Finally, copy *Rain Forest Facts* and *Rain Forest Facts About Trees* on page 103 and tape them to your door if there is space.

The Walls

Encourage your students to "leap into learning" right from day one. To make this display, cover your bulletin board with brown paper. Copy the reproducibles on pages 123-125 and have children color them. Color the frogs in stripe and spot patterns using the brightest colors in the crayon box. Add *Rain Forest Facts About Poison Dart Frogs* on page 103 to the board.

The Walls

This toucan can spell and so can your kids! Trace the body of the toucan on page 126 onto black paper. Trace the toucan's face onto yellow paper. Trace the beak onto white paper and color it using red, orange, blue and green. Assemble the parts of the toucan on your bulletin board. Add the heading and speech balloon on pages 126-127 and *Rain Forest Facts About Birds* on page 104.

The Walls

This multipurpose, interactive display teaches children about weather conditions here and in the rain forest. It also gives practice in reading a thermometer and gets them in the habit of looking at a newspaper every day. Copy the weather symbols on page 128 and mount them on a circle of oaktag. Cut three arrows out of oaktag. Copy the thermometer on page 128 and heading on page 127 and *Rain Forest Facts About the Weather* on page 104.

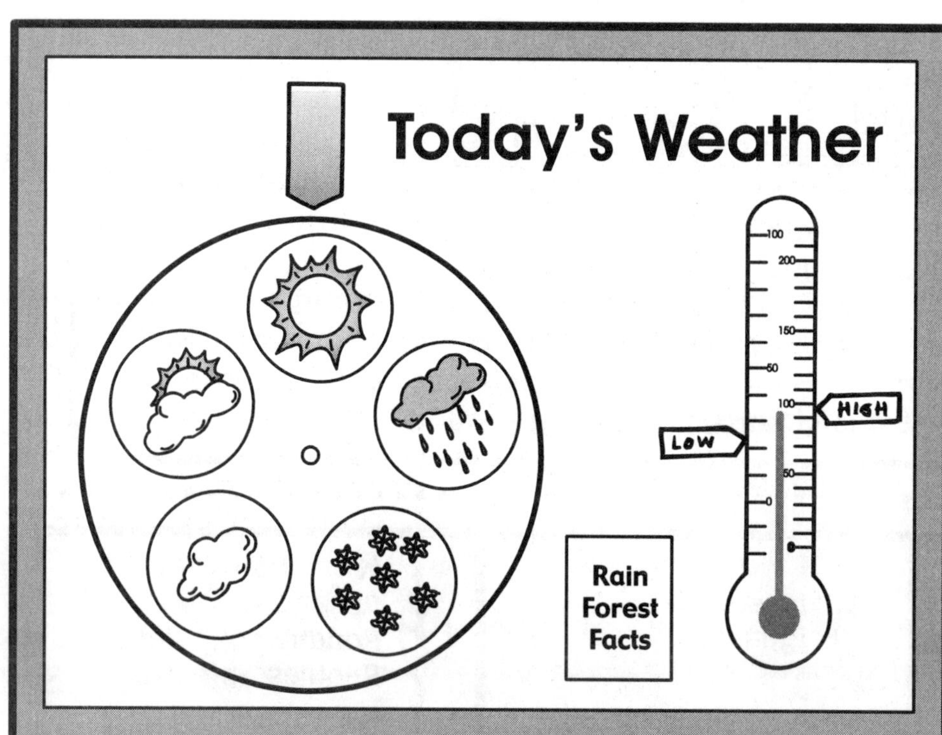

Have your students start each morning with a quick check of the day's high and low temperatures in your local paper. Have them use the arrows to mark the highs and lows on the thermometer and turn the weather wheel so that the day's forecast lines up with the arrow. Take this opportunity to teach older children about Fahrenheit and Celsius.

The Walls

This light-hearted birthday bulletin board with its fanciful play on words will make children chuckle. Copy the iguana and iguana's speech balloon on page 129 and the cake and candles on page 130. Write the birthday children's names and birthdays on the candles. Write the month at the top of the board. Add *Rain Forest Facts About Iguanas* on page 104 for a quick lesson about this favorite reptile, as well as *Rain Forest Facts About Food & Medicine*.

The Walls

Encircle your room with a glorious, colorful rain forest frieze! Assign a letter to each child. Have the children illustrate something associated with the rain forest that begins with their letter. Choose words from this list or come up with your own. Have children write a sentence or two about their rain forest words on their papers. Hang pictures in alphabetical order, side by side, along the top of the chalkboard, continuing around the room.

A
Amazon
Anacondas
Anteaters

B
Birds
Bats
Butterflies

C
Camouflage
Canopy
Crocodile

D
Drugs
Diversity
Deforestation

E
Emergent layer
Eagles
Ecology

F
Fruit
Flowers
Food chain

G
Geckos
Gorillas

H
Hummingbirds
Howler monkeys
Habitat

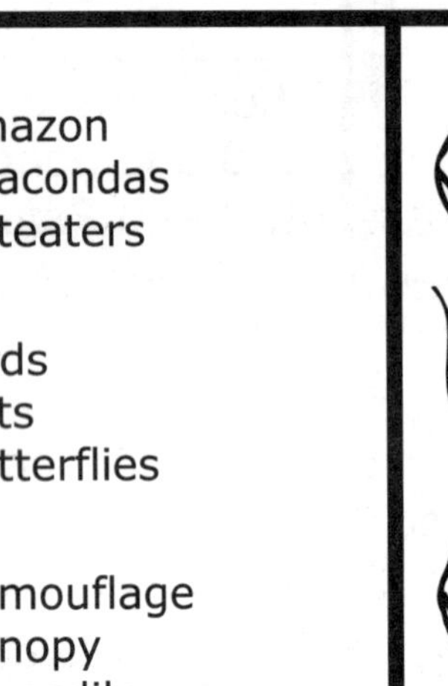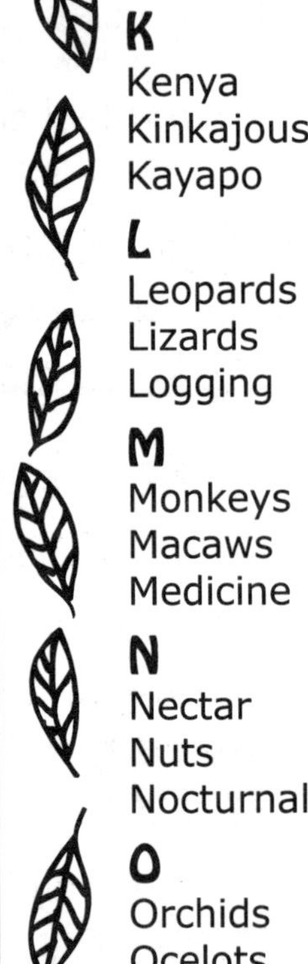

I
Insects
Iguanas

J
Jaguars
Jungle cats

K
Kenya
Kinkajous
Kayapo

L
Leopards
Lizards
Logging

M
Monkeys
Macaws
Medicine

N
Nectar
Nuts
Nocturnal

O
Orchids
Ocelots
Orangutans

P
Parrots
Piranhas
Plants

Q
eQuator
Quetzals

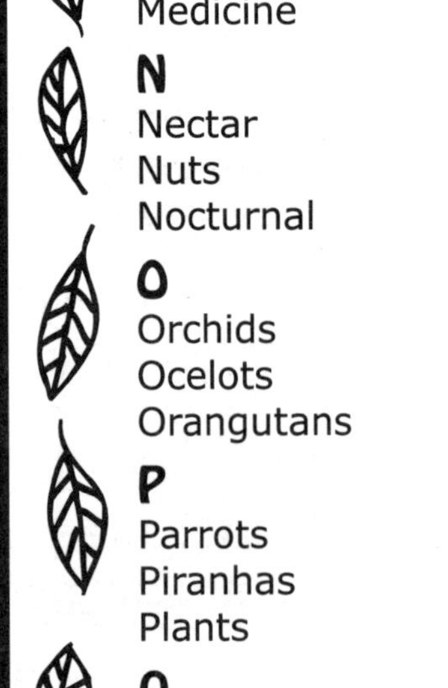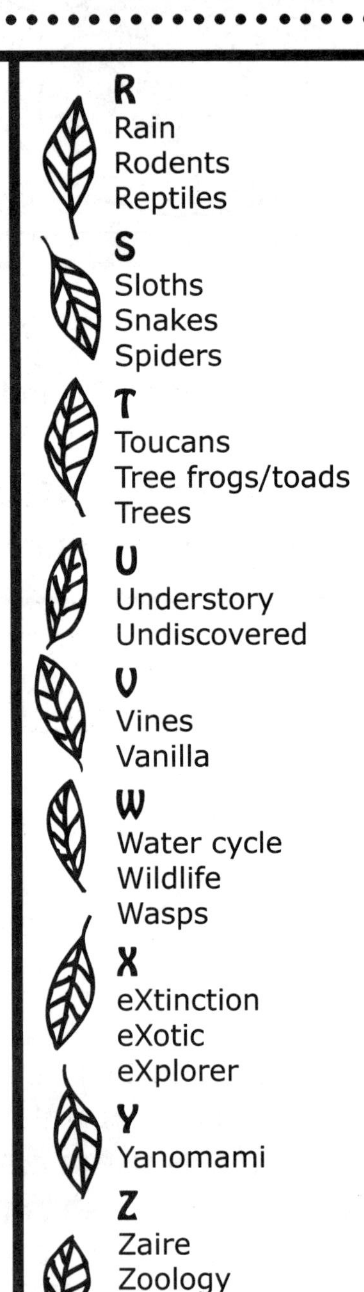

R
Rain
Rodents
Reptiles

S
Sloths
Snakes
Spiders

T
Toucans
Tree frogs/toads
Trees

U
Understory
Undiscovered

V
Vines
Vanilla

W
Water cycle
Wildlife
Wasps

X
eXtinction
eXotic
eXplorer

Y
Yanomami

Z
Zaire
Zoology

The Walls

Rain Forest Fact Cards open children's eyes to the wonders of this magical place. Feel free to copy the cards and place them on your bulletin boards, chalkboards, doors, above a water fountain or sink, or anywhere around the building.

Rain Forest Facts

- Millions of animal and plant species live in the rain forest. Most of them haven't even been discovered yet!

- The rain forest is home to mammals. Gorillas live in the rain forests of Africa. Orangutans are found in Asia. A sloth is a slow-moving mammal of South America. Insects and algae live in its fur.

- Pythons, boa constrictors and anacondas are giant snakes. Some grow 30 feet long and weigh 200 pounds. They eat birds, pigs and even crocodiles.

- The rain forest is home to people too. Many live the same way their ancestors did thousands of years ago.

Rain Forest Facts About Trees

- Some trees in the rain forest grow as high as a 20-story building.

- Almost half of the tropical rain forests have been destroyed by humans.

- When the trees are cut down, the plants and animals that depend on the trees also die. Many species are already extinct, even before they have been discovered.

Rain Forest Facts About Poison Dart Frogs

- Poison dart frogs can be red, orange, yellow, purple or green, with stripes and spots on their bodies.

- They have a deadly poison in their skin. Their bright colors warn other animals to stay away. South American Indians put the poison on their darts and arrows.

- Poison dart tadpoles live in little pools of water formed by the leaves of the bromeliad plant.

The Walls

<table>
<tr><td>

Rain Forest Facts About Birds

- The rain forest is home to 2600 kinds of birds, nearly $1/3$ of all bird species on Earth.
- Toucans don't build nests. They live in tree holes.
- A toucan's bill can be as long as its body. Because the bill is hollow, it is not heavy.

</td><td>

Rain Forest Facts About Weather

- The temperature in tropical rain forests is about 80°F (27°C) every day. It is always hot, humid and rainy.
- Rain forests get between 100" (254 cm) and 400" (1016 cm) of rain every year.
- It rains nearly every afternoon, sometimes as much as 5" (12.7 cm) at one time.
- There are plants in the rain forest whose leaves are so big they can be used as umbrellas!

</td></tr>
<tr><td>

Rain Forest Facts About Iguanas

- Iguanas are lizards. They are less than 12" (30.48 cm) at birth, but can grow up to 6 feet (182.88 cm) as adults.
- Iguanas can live for 30 years.
- They are excellent runners, climbers and swimmers.

</td><td>

Rain Forest Facts About Food & Medicine

- Next time you eat a slice of birthday cake, remember, chocolate and vanilla grow in the rain forest.
- Pineapples, mangoes, cinnamon, bananas, sugar, coffee, tea and many kinds of nuts are also native to the rain forest.
- Medicines from rain forest plants have helped people with cancer, malaria, whooping cough, glaucoma and other diseases. Many other rain forest medicines are still waiting to be discovered.

</td></tr>
</table>

The Desks

___________'s

Folder

To do:

- ☐ 1. _______________________
- ☐ 2. _______________________
- ☐ 3. _______________________
- ☐ 4. _______________________
- ☐ 5. _______________________

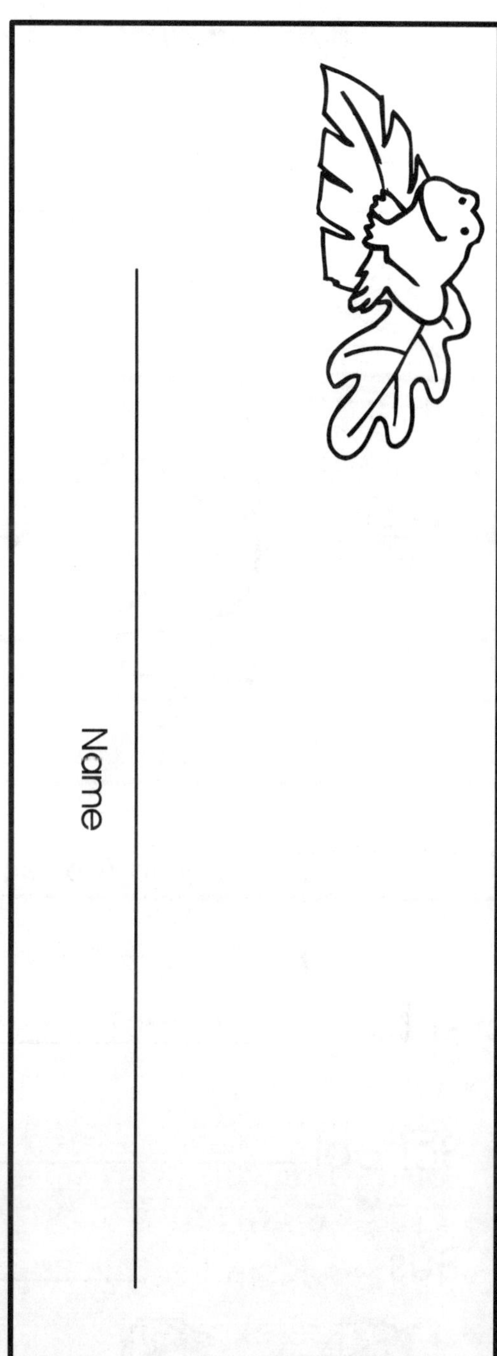

Folder Label: Glue a label on a file folder for each child. Use folders for in-class assignments and homework. Use the checklist to keep track of student work.

Desk Name Tag: Fold a 5¹/₂"x 7" (13.95 x 17.78 cm) piece of oaktag in half, lengthwise. Mount name tag on oaktag.

The Children

My name is

____

____
Name

Name _______________

School _______________

Bus _______________

The Awards & Rewards

_______________ knows how

to follow directions!

Signed _______________

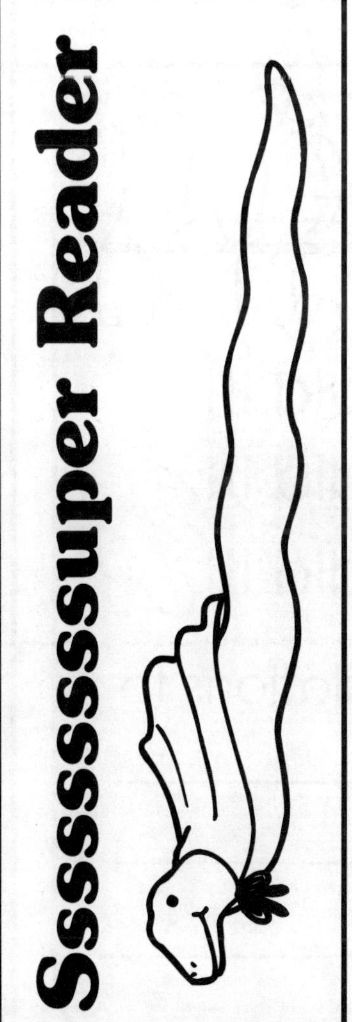

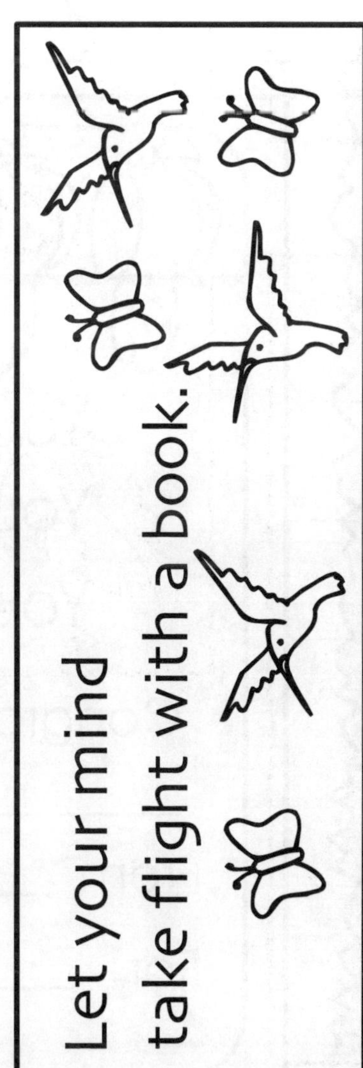

The Awards & Rewards

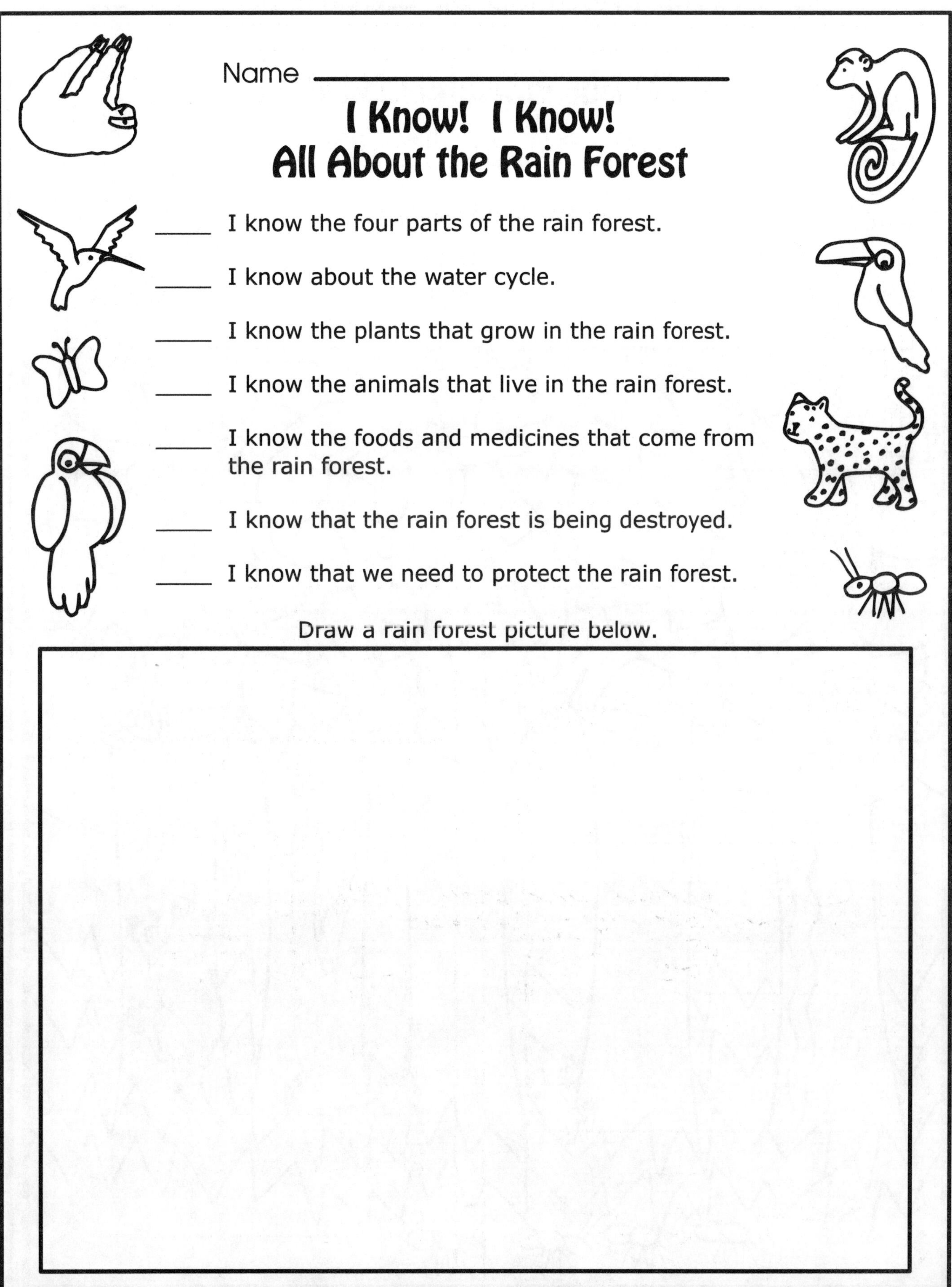

Name _______________________________

I Know! I Know!
All About the Rain Forest

_____ I know the four parts of the rain forest.

_____ I know about the water cycle.

_____ I know the plants that grow in the rain forest.

_____ I know the animals that live in the rain forest.

_____ I know the foods and medicines that come from the rain forest.

_____ I know that the rain forest is being destroyed.

_____ I know that we need to protect the rain forest.

Draw a rain forest picture below.

Rain Forest Hide-and-Seek

Look for these rain forest creatures hiding in the picture.
Color the ones that you find.

tree frog	sloth	toucan	butterfly
snake	parrot	leopard	hummingbird
crocodile	iguana	ants	spider monkey

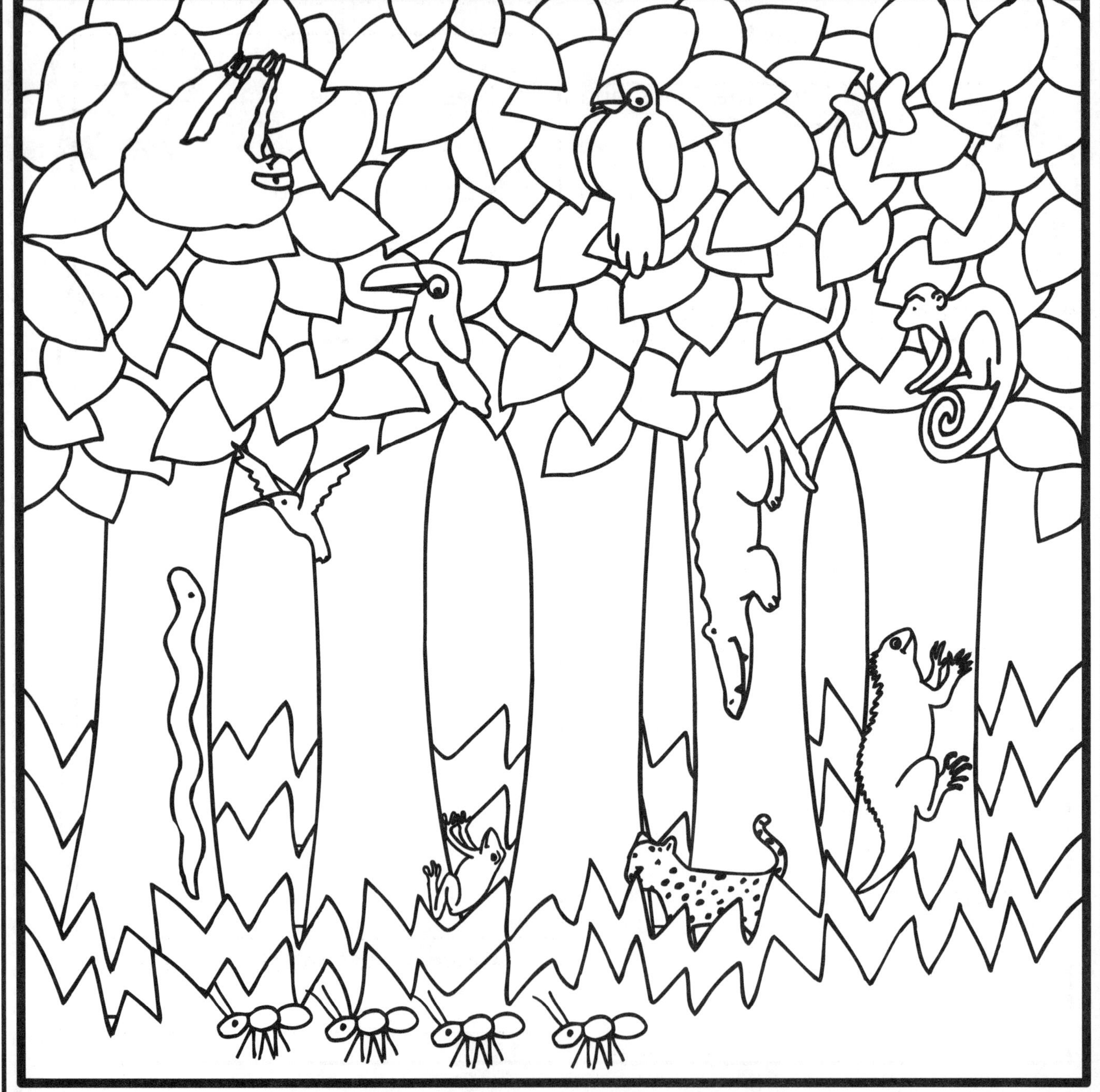

The Rain Forest News

New Species Found in the Rain Forest!

Explorer _________________________ has discovered a new rain forest animal.
your name

It is called a ____.

It eats _______________________________

_______________________________.

It lives in a _______________________.

Here are three things it can do:

____

____

____

____

____

____

Above is the first picture of a

_______________________________.

The Books & Media

Rain Forest Books

Crafts for Kids Who Are Wild About Rain Forests
by Kathy Ross, Econo-Clad Books, 1999.
twenty projects with step-by-step instructions, using recycled and inexpensive materials.

A Teacher's Guide to a Walk in the Rainforest by Bruce and Carol Malnor, Dawn Publications, 1998.
An easy-to-follow, well-organized activity resource. Offers several modes of learning, including the body, feelings and the intellect.

Nature's Green Umbrella: Tropical Rain Forests
by Gail Gibbons, Mulberry Books, 1997.
Bright, colorful watercolors and text explain the complex ecosystem of rain forests and their importance to global ecology.

Here Is the Tropical Rain Forest
by Madeleine Dunphy, Hyperion, 1997.
In a "this is the house that Jack built" format, the text with its distinctive rhythm links plants, animals and climate. The frog who bathes in the rain is protected by the bromeliad which is held by the tree, and so on.

Look Closer: Rain Forest
by Barbara Taylor and Frank Greenaway, DK Publishing, 1998.
Engagingly presented information and bright photographs give a real sense of where each plant or creature lives, how it eats, breeds, survives and adapts.

At Home in the Rain Forest
by Diane Willow, Charlesbridge Publishing, 1992.
From the tops of tropical trees to the forest floor, readers observe the interrelationships of plants and animals that thrive at each level of the rain forest.

Rain Forest Birds
by Bobbie Kalman, Crabtree Publishing, 1998.
This colorful book introduces unique and beautiful birds, from the scarlet-feathered macaw to the monkey-eating eagle.

Beneath the Canopy
by Kevin Schafer, Chronicle Books, 1999.
A photographic close-up of rare wildlife in the Latin American rain forest, including the glass frog, giant river otter and mountain paca.

The Great Kapok Tree
by Lynn Cherry, Harcourt, 2000.
An exceptionally colorful book explains the importance of the kapok tree to the creatures that call it home, and the importance of rain forests to the world's ecology.

Videos

The Magic School Bus in the Rain Forest
Scholastic, 1999.
When Ms. Frizzle's cocoa tree for Earth Day bears only one pod, the investigation of a rain forest plant begins. With chocolate as the "pull," the video illustrates how pods, mud puddles and bugs play a role in the plant's development.

National Geographic Rain Forest, 1983.
See a deadly snake snatch a drink, a mother sloth take her young for a walk, a colony of ants defend its home from encroaching vines, grasshoppers and more.

Web Sites

rainforest-alliance.org
A colorful, kid-friendly, award-winning site full of resources, facts and links. Includes classroom activities. Worth a visit!

worldwildlife.org
Visit the Critter of the Day, endangered species and forests with this easy-to-use site from the World Wildlife Fund.

Chocolate-Dipped Bananas

For this easy-to-prepare recipe using two rain forest foods, you'll need:

1/2 banana per student
2 oz. chocolate per each 1/2 banana
craft sticks
double boiler
wax paper
cookie sheet

- Peel each banana and cut in half crosswise. Insert a stick into the flat end of each half.

- Melt chocolate in a double boiler with water in the bottom pan. Let chocolate cool 4-5 minutes.

- Have children dip a banana half into the melted chocolate, turning to coat it.

- Put bananas on a wax paper-lined cookie sheet and place in the freezer.

- Freeze bananas for about one hour. Let thaw for 10 minutes before eating.

Cool Rain Forest Brew

It's hot in the rain forest! Cool off by making this tropical fruit brew. For 20-24 children, you'll need:

6 cups apricot nectar
6 cups orange or
    pineapple juice
4 cups orange sherbet
2 quarts ginger ale
large bowl

- Combine apricot nectar and orange or pineapple juice in large bowl.

- Add ginger ale just before serving.

- Pour into large cups and add a small scoop of orange sherbet.

Cucumber Crocodile

To create this cute group snack, you'll need:

1 large cucumber
2 green olives stuffed with pimentos
4 baby carrots
1 can of pineapple chunks
1 block of cheese cut into cubes
toothpicks
knife

- Have an adult cut a zigzag mouth in the more rounded end of the cucumber.

- Slice off the top of each baby carrot. Insert a toothpick into the flat end of each carrot and then insert the rest of the toothpick into the cucumber, creating four legs.

- Place each olive on a toothpick and insert into the cucumber for the crocodile's eyes.

- Have each student put a cheese cube and a pineapple chunk on a toothpick and insert into the crocodile's back.

- After admiring the crocodile, have each child remove a toothpick treat. Slice cucumber and serve.

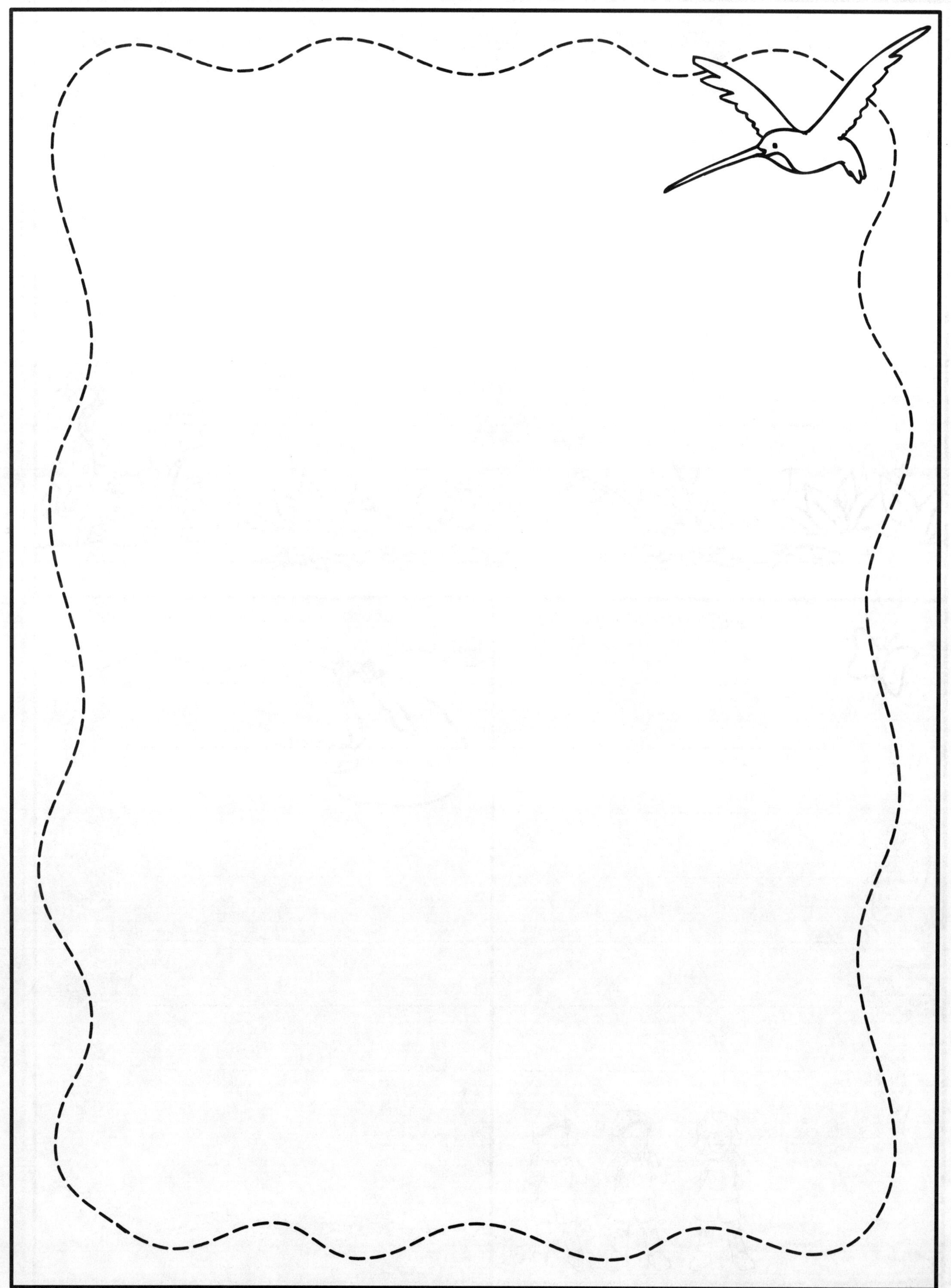

The Clip Art

The Clip Art

Rain
Forest
Explorers

The Reproducibles

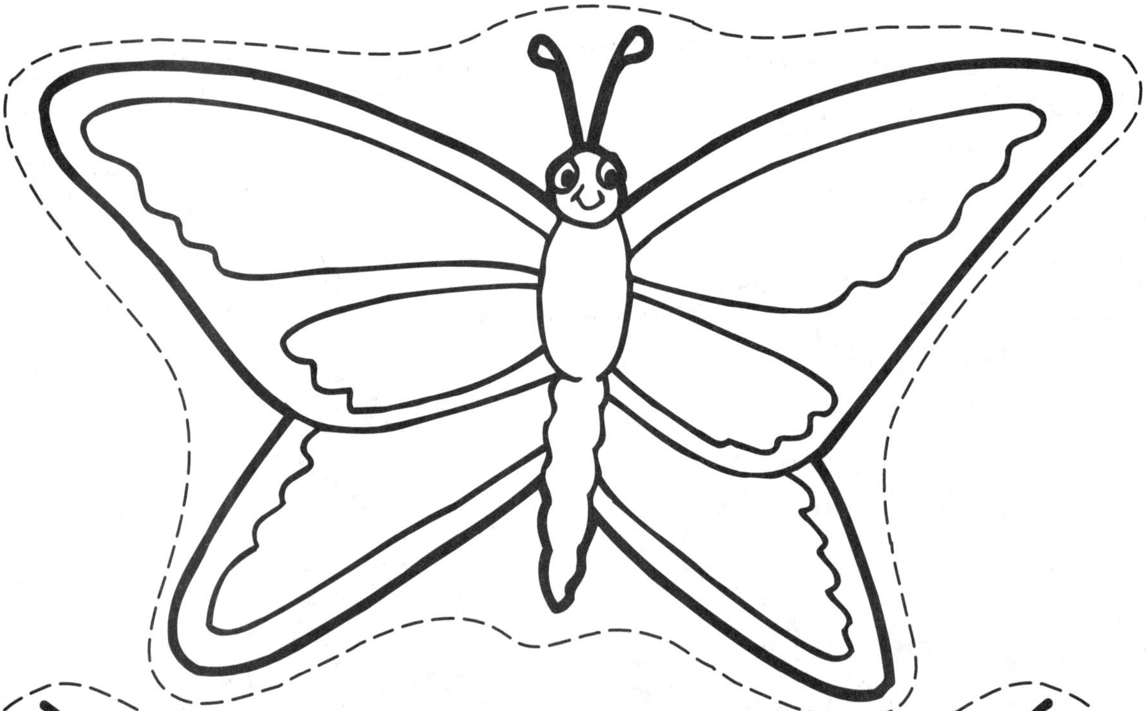

The Reproducibles

The Reproducibles

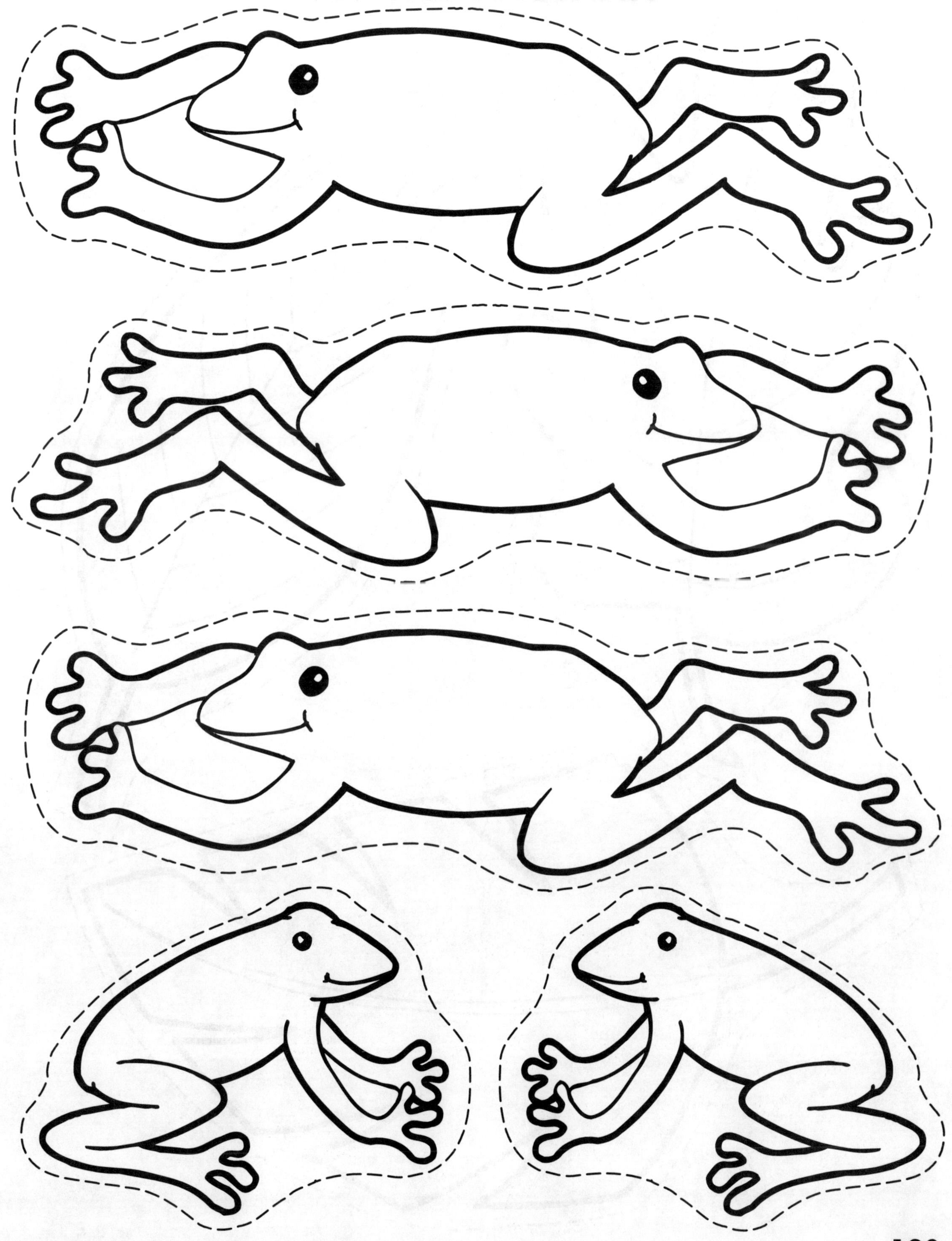

The Reproducibles

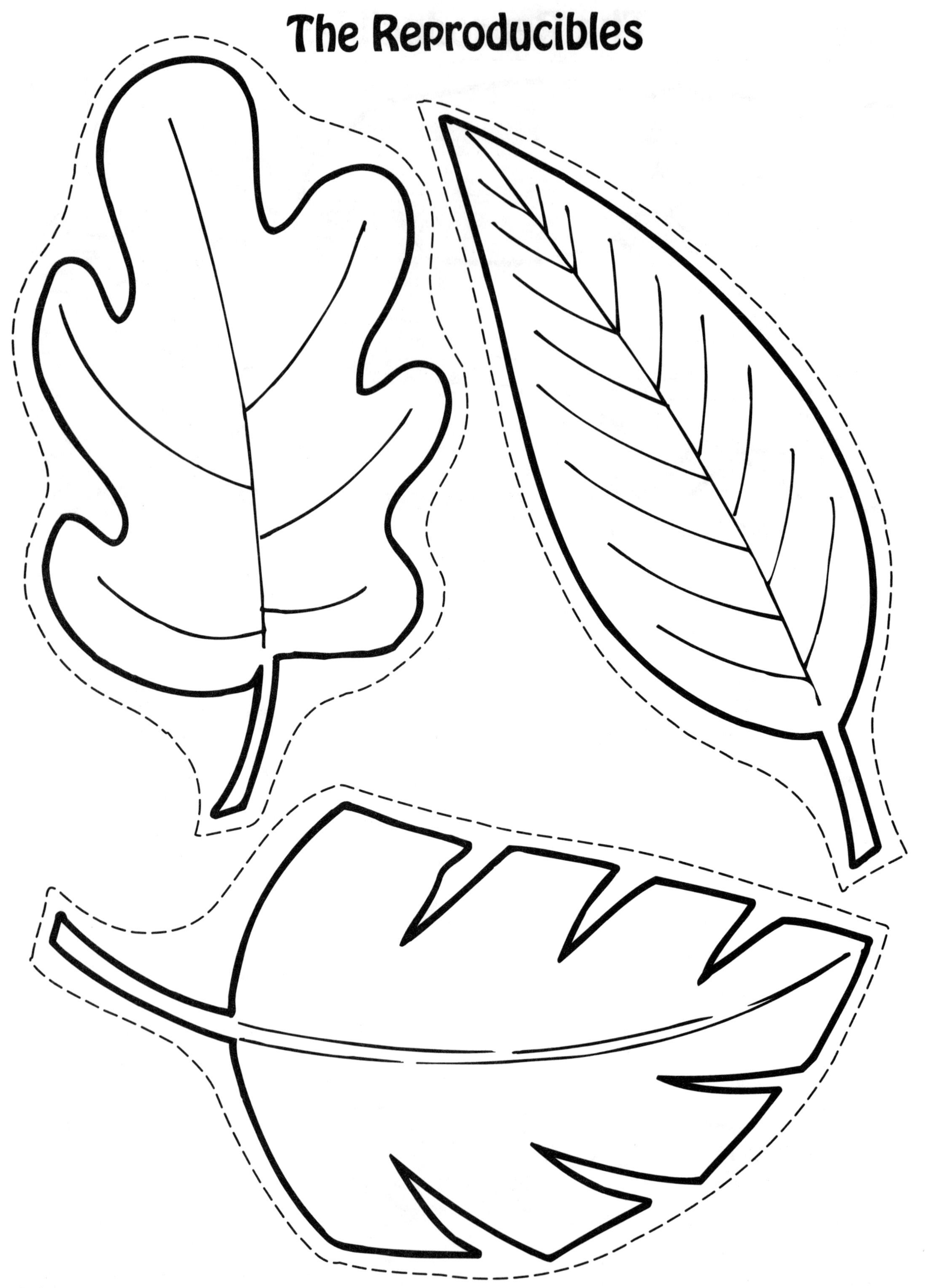

Leap into Learning!

I too can spell!

We can

Spell!

Today's

Weather

The Reproducibles

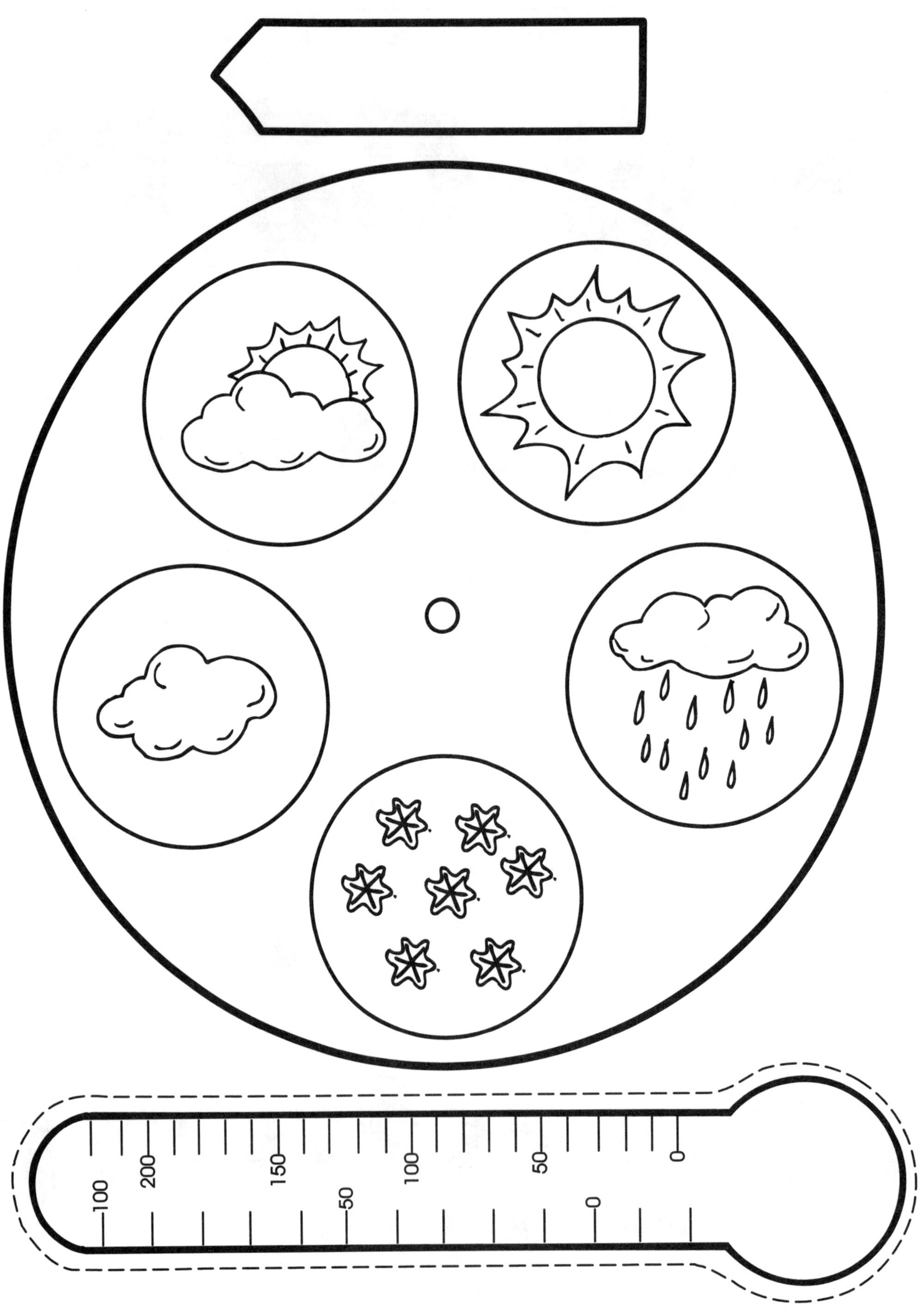

Iguana wish
you a
Happy Birthday!

The Reproducibles

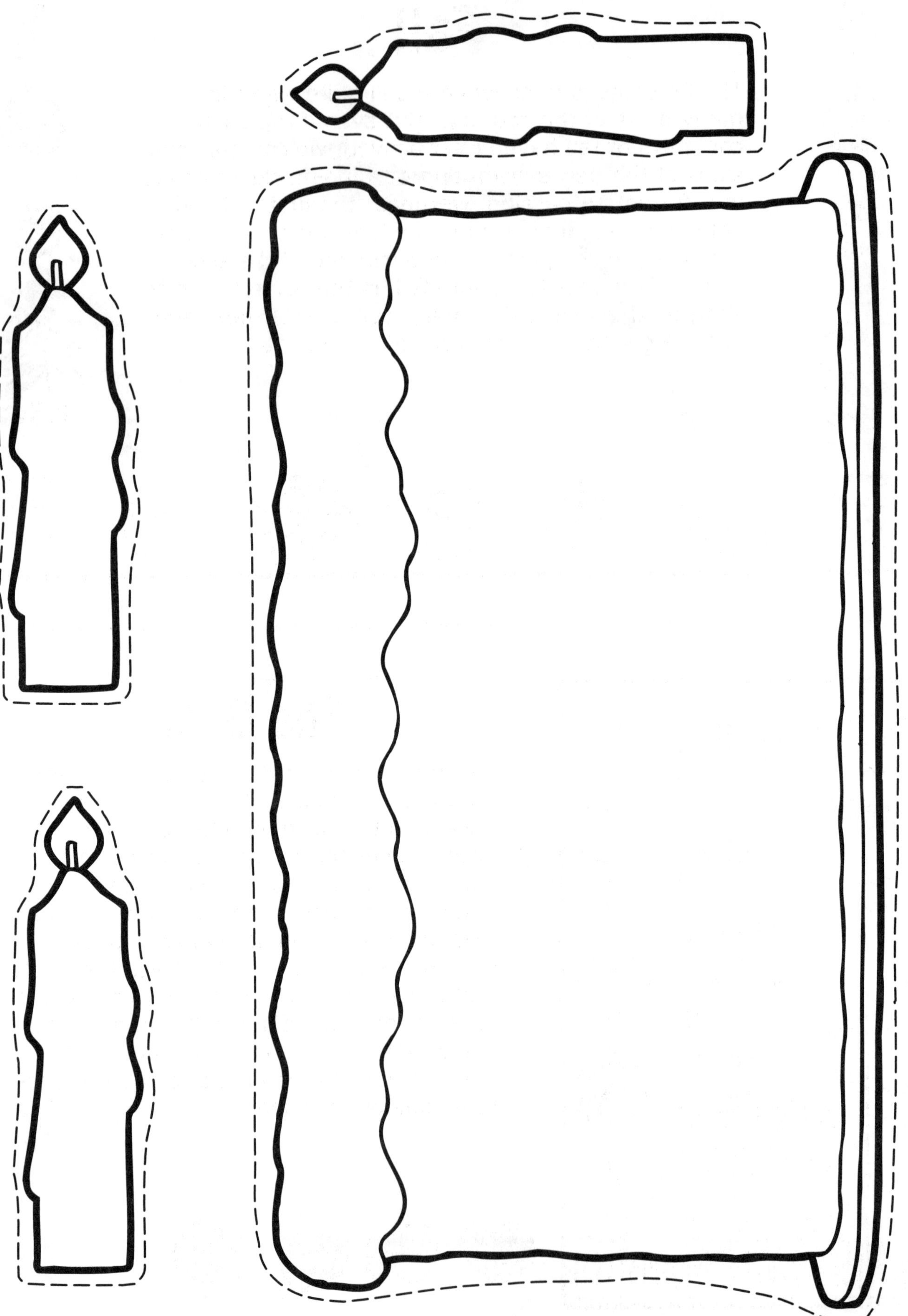

Fall

The first weeks of school are still quite warm in many parts of the country. But even if the crisp, cool days of fall haven't yet arrived, we can still spot signs of the new season approaching–flocks of geese in V-formation passing overhead; the first red and golden leaves appearing in the trees; orchards heavy with ripe, juicy apples. The beginning of the school year, as summer turns into fall, is the perfect time to sharpen the senses–to smell, touch, taste, hear and see the changes taking place all around us.

The Door

Welcome children with cheery apples and an upbeat message. To make the apple basket, cut strips of butcher paper or brown paper bags. Arrange strips as shown in the illustration and trim the edges into a basket shape. Crumple and twist a piece of butcher paper or paper bags to create the branch. Trace the apple patterns on page 150 onto red, yellow and green paper. Write a child's name on each apple. Copy the heading on page 149. Add a fringe of green paper along the bottom edge of your door.

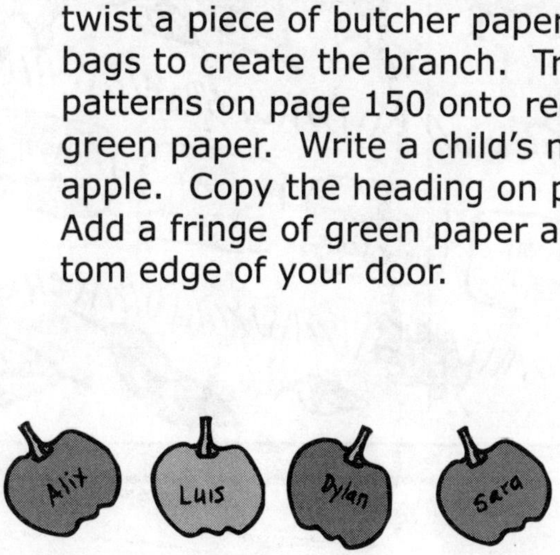

The Windows

Colorful fall suncatchers capture the spirit of the season. Arrange leaves, maple seed pods, evergreen needles, dried grasses and other flat items from nature on a sheet of waxed paper. Grate fall-colored crayons and scatter shavings over the items. Sprinkle on a little bit of glitter. Put another sheet of waxed paper on top and press with a warm iron for a few seconds, allowing the crayon shavings to melt and the edges to seal. Trim collages, mount them on your windows and see how they catch the sun.

The Walls

A few simple guidelines can make the "learning path" a lot smoother. Copy the heading on page 151. Cut stepping-stones out of brown paper. Create and cut out your own "smart steps" and attach them to the stones. Trace the leaf patterns on page 154 onto red, orange and yellow paper. Copy or trace the birds and animals on pages 152 and 153 and add them to your display.

The Walls

Just as the farmer's hard work leads to a bountiful harvest, your students' hard work reaps a crop of good ideas. To make this display, copy the heading on page 151. Glue unpopped popcorn kernels on oaktag cut into the shape of corncobs. Cut up real corn husks or green paper for stalks and leaves. Copy and color the reproducibles on pages 152-156.

The Walls

Share your enthusiasm for learning and your pride in student achievement. You may adapt this display for any subject, from spelling to science. Using super glue, attach acorns, horse chestnuts and any other nuts you find in your neighborhood to strands of yarn. Dry thoroughly. Copy the heading on page 157 and the characters on pages 152-153.

The Walls

The beautiful fall season is the perfect time for a nature walk. Give each child a bag or box in which to collect pretty leaves, pinecones, acorns, nuts, seed pods, dried grasses and wildflowers, evergreen needles, feathers and interesting stones. Back in the classroom, press leaves overnight between the pages of a heavy book. Then display your fall finds on this unusual bulletin board, following the instructions above. Add the heading on page 158.

The Walls

Here's a delightful way to manage classroom chores. Copy the characters on pages 160-161 and color them in. Write a job on each apple. When assigning chores, write the child's name on an apple leaf cut from green paper and pin it to the appropriate apple. Add the heading from page 159.

The Desks

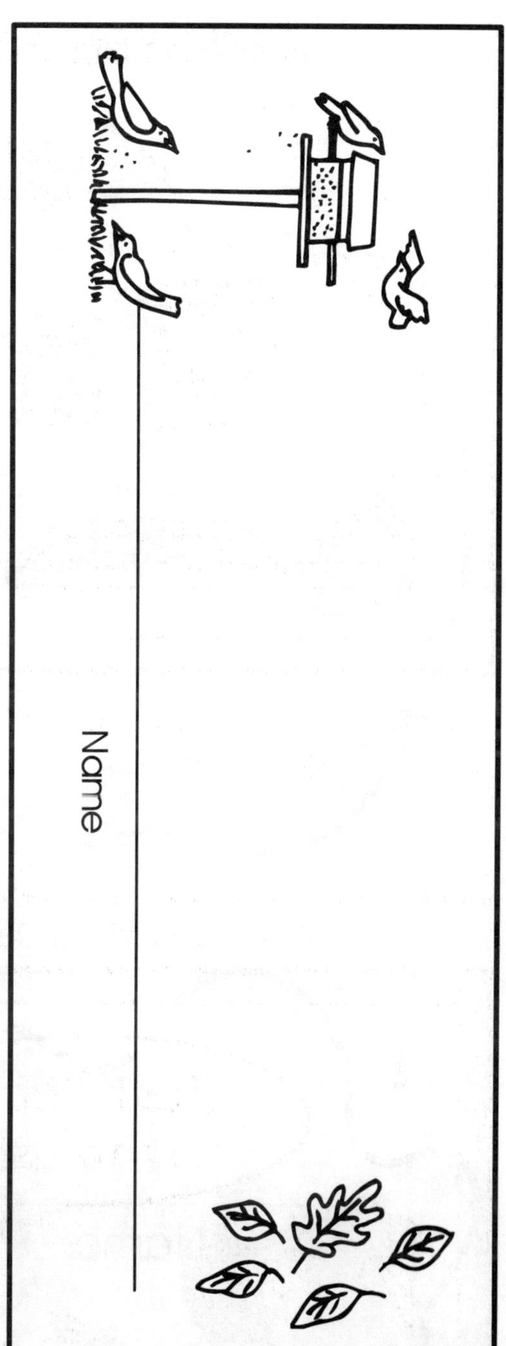

Folder Label: Glue a label on a file folder for each child. Use folders for in-class assignments and homework. Use the checklist to keep track of student work.

Desk Name Tag: Fold a 5$\frac{1}{2}$" x 7" (13.95 x 17.78 cm) piece of oaktag in half, lengthwise. Mount name tag on oaktag.

The Children

The Awards & Rewards

Creative Kid Award

To _________________________

From _______________________

For ________________________

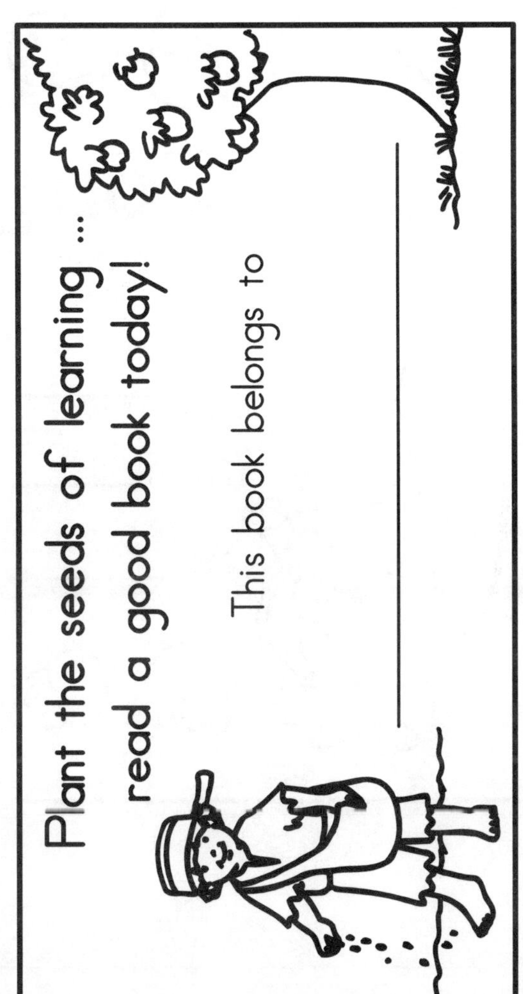

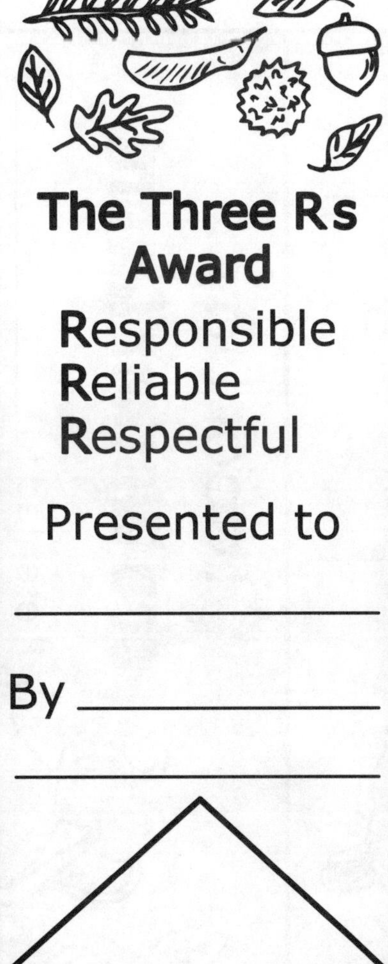

Congratulations
on your BIG success!
To
From
For
is off to a good start in
.
Signed
Labor Day
Good Worker Award
Presented to
From
For

I Know! I Know!
All About Fall

_____ I know what the weather is like in fall.

_____ I know why leaves change color in fall.

_____ I know why trees drop their leaves in fall.

_____ I know what animals do in fall.

_____ I know where birds go in fall.

_____ I know many fruits and vegetables that ripen in fall.

_____ I know that the days grow shorter and the nights grow longer in fall.

Draw a fall picture below.

Fall Leaves

Think about fall leaves. What do they look like? How do they smell? Do they make a sound? What do they feel like when you touch them? What happens to leaves in the fall? How do fall leaves make you feel?

Fill the leaf with words that describe fall leaves.

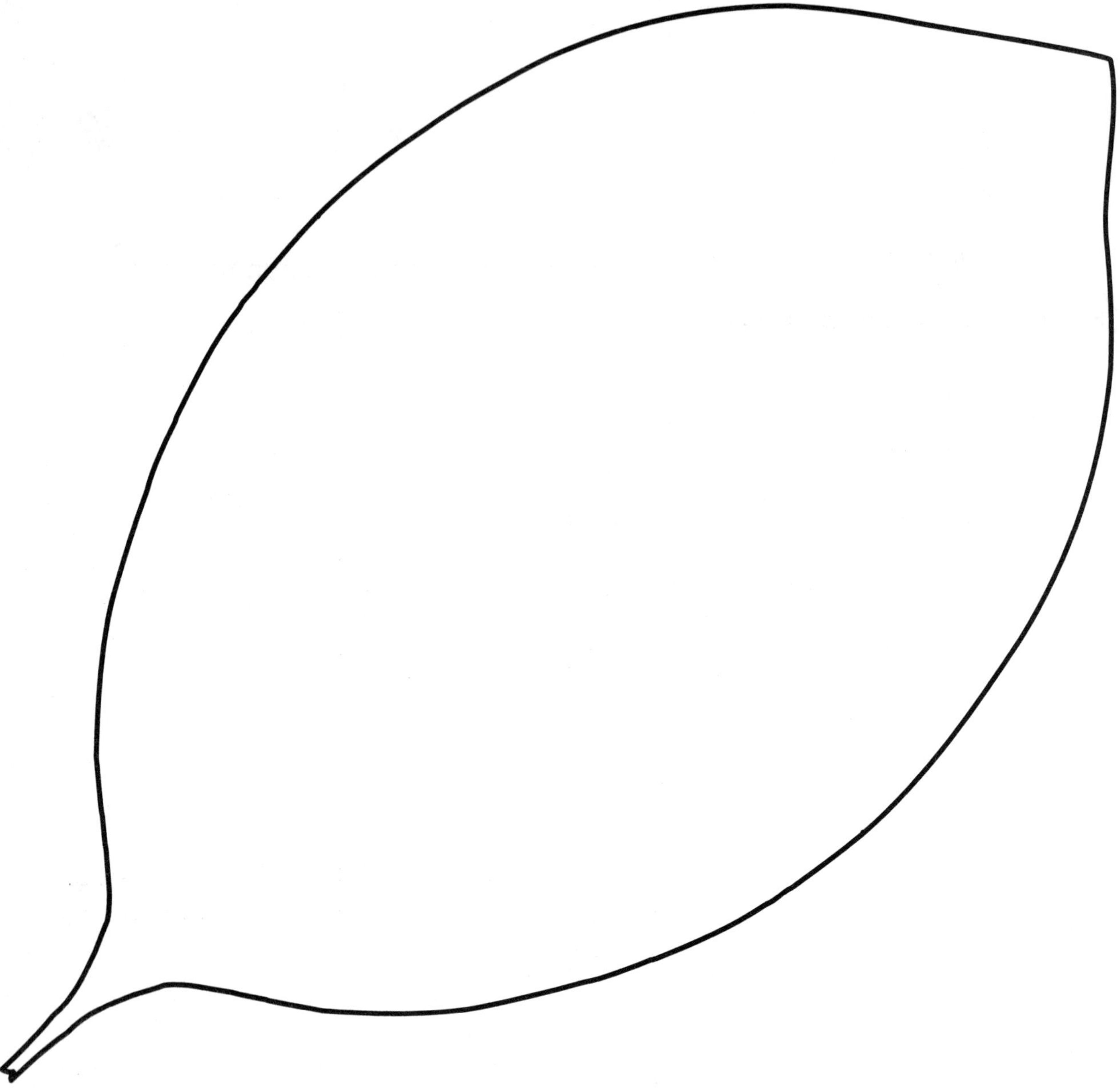

Now use some of your words to write a poem about fall leaves. (Your poem does not have to rhyme.) Cut a piece of red, yellow or orange paper into the shape of a leaf. Paste your poem on the leaf.

Signs of the Seasons

Your can be a nature watcher! Keep your eyes open for the changes that take place in the fall. If you spot any of these fall events, write down the date.

Red leaves ____

Yellow leaves ____

Orange leaves ____

Falling leaves ____

A big pile of leaves ______________________________________

A person raking leaves ___________________________________

Birds flying south in V-formation ________________________

Acorns or other nuts on the ground ______________________

A squirrel gathering food ________________________________

Ripe apples on a tree or in a farmer's market __________

Ripe pumpkins in a garden or farmer's market _________

Indian corn and gourds in a garden or farmer's market _____

A monarch butterfly flying south _________________________

A harvest moon (the full moon in September) ___________

A very windy day ____

A chilly day ____

The first frost ____

Other signs of the season in your neighborhood _________

____

____

____

The Books & Media

Fall Books

Apples by Elaine Landau, Children's Press, 1999.
This book gives an easy-to-understand overview of apples, their history, cultivation and uses, and describes several of the most popular varieties.

Applesauce
by Shirley Kurtz, Good Books, 1992.
The happy story of a family who works together to make enough applesauce to last through the coming winter. Includes directions for canning applesauce.

Hooray for Orchards
by Bobbie Kalman, Crabtree, 1997.
An introduction to orchards and the development, harvesting and processing of apples.

The Seasons of Arnold's Apple Tree
by Gail Gibbons, Voyager, 1984.
As the seasons pass, a boy enjoys a variety of activities, thanks to his apple tree.

Apples and Pumpkins
by Anne Rockwell, Simon & Schuster, 1994.
A joyful adventure of a young girl and her parents as they go to a farm to pick apples and pumpkins. Bold, autumn-colored illustrations enrich this simple but lively story.

Johnny Appleseed: A Tall Tale
by Steven Kellogg, William Morrow, 1998.
Marvelous illustrations combine history with the legends surrounding John Chapman. Wherever he roamed, Chapman cleared land to plant apple trees, earning the fond name Johnny Appleseed.

Why Do Leaves Change Colors?
by Betsy Maestro, HarperCollins, 1994.
Explains how leaves change color in autumn and then fall to the ground as the tree prepares for winter. Includes clear illustrations and identification of various leaves.

Autumn Leaves
by Ken Robbins, Scholastic, 1998.
The shapes and characteristics of leaves from 13 deciduous trees are explored on two-page spreads with crisp, colorful, life-size photos and simple text.

The Tremendous Tree Book
by Barbara Brenner and May Garelick, Boyds Mills, 1979.
A new version of an old favorite told in simple rhyme with verses that celebrate the marvels of trees. Cut-paper illustrations add an interesting artistic touch to each page.

It Could Still Be a Leaf
by Allan Fowler, Children's Press, 1993.
An easy, read-aloud book with brilliant photos about different kinds of leaves, their forms and colors.

The Autumn Equinox: Celebrating the Harvest
by Ellen Jackson, Millbrook, 2000.
The significance of harvest festivals around the world are described and illustrated with classroom activities that include games, crafts and recipes.

Possum's Harvest Moon
by Ann Hunter, Houghton Miffin, 1996.
Possum wakes up one autumn evening and decides to invite his animal friends to a party to celebrate the beautiful harvest moon one last time before the long winter. A quiet story.

Crafts to Make in the Fall
by Kathy Ross, Millbrook, 1998.
Presents 29 craft projects including a soft sculpture pumpkin, a changing tree puppet, a school bus picture frame and a fall tree label pin.

Music

The Four Seasons by Antonio Vivaldi.
Play any recording of this beloved string concert for your class. Each movement conveys the mood of a different season. Listen for sounds of the hunt in autumn.

Web Site

freefoto.com/pictures/nature/autumn2/index.asp
Create a fall landscape using this wide selection of color photographs you may print for free for classroom use.

Apple Smoothies

Here's a refreshing treat for those hot back-to-school days. For four six-ounce servings, you'll need:

2 8-ounce cartons of low-fat apple yogurt
1 6-ounce can of frozen apple juice concentrate
4 ice cubes

- Put each of the ingredients, in the order listed, in a blender.
- Blend until smooth and creamy.

Pumpkin Muffins

Serve Pumpkin Muffins with Apple Smoothies or a cup of cider for a healthy welcome-back-to-school breakfast or snack. For 12 muffins, you'll need:

1 cup canned pumpkin
$1/2$ cup packed brown sugar
$1/4$ cup melted butter
2 eggs
$3/4$ cup milk
2 cups flour
2 teaspoons baking soda
$1/2$ teaspoon salt

- Mix the first four ingredients in a large bowl. Add milk.
- Mix flour, baking soda and salt in a separate bowl.
- Add to pumpkin mixture. Blend, but do not overmix.
- Bake in paper liners in a muffin tin at 375°F for 20 minutes.

The Clip Art

The Clip Art

We're off to a good start!

The Reproducibles

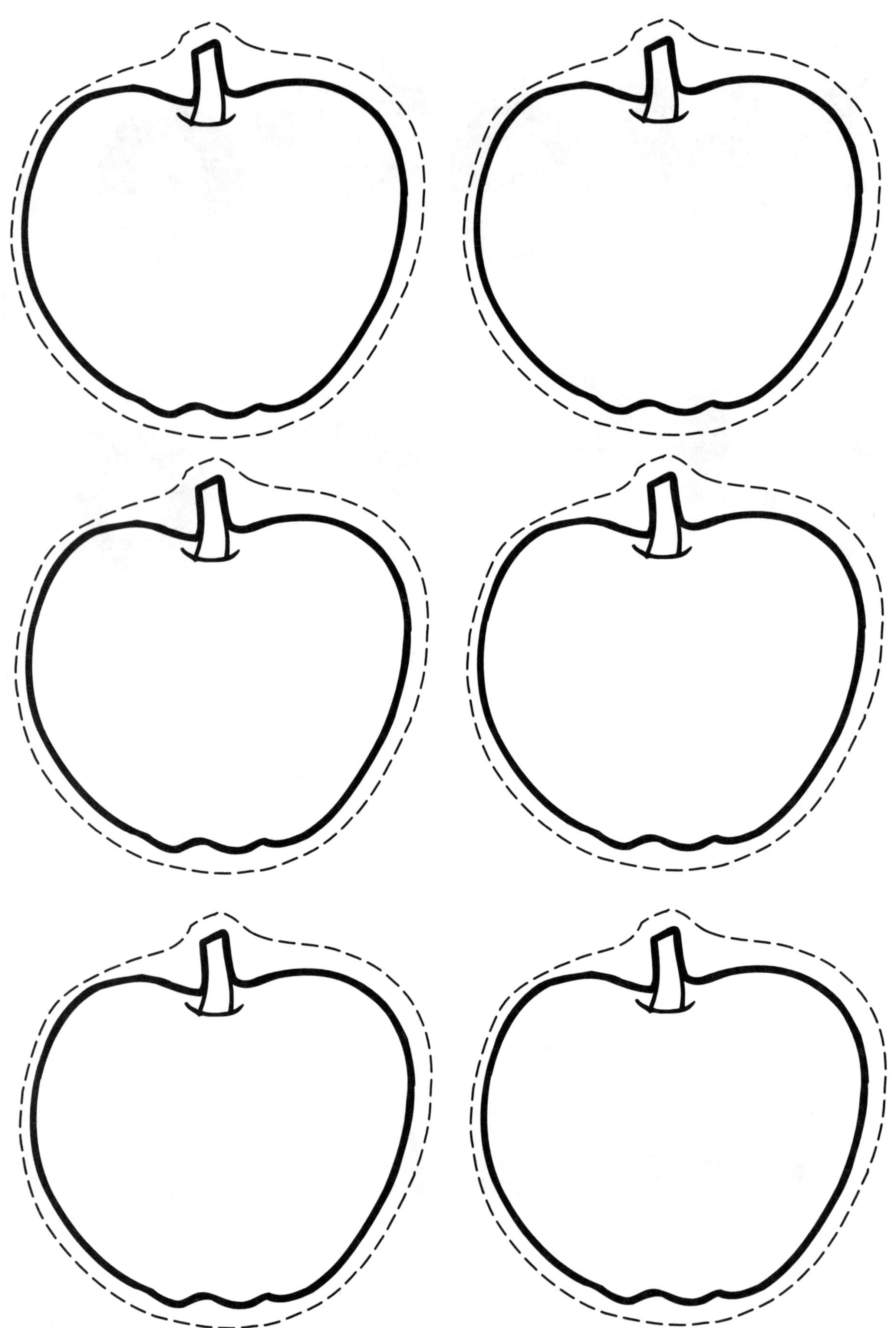

Smart steps on the path to learning.

A harvest of good ideas.

The Reproducibles

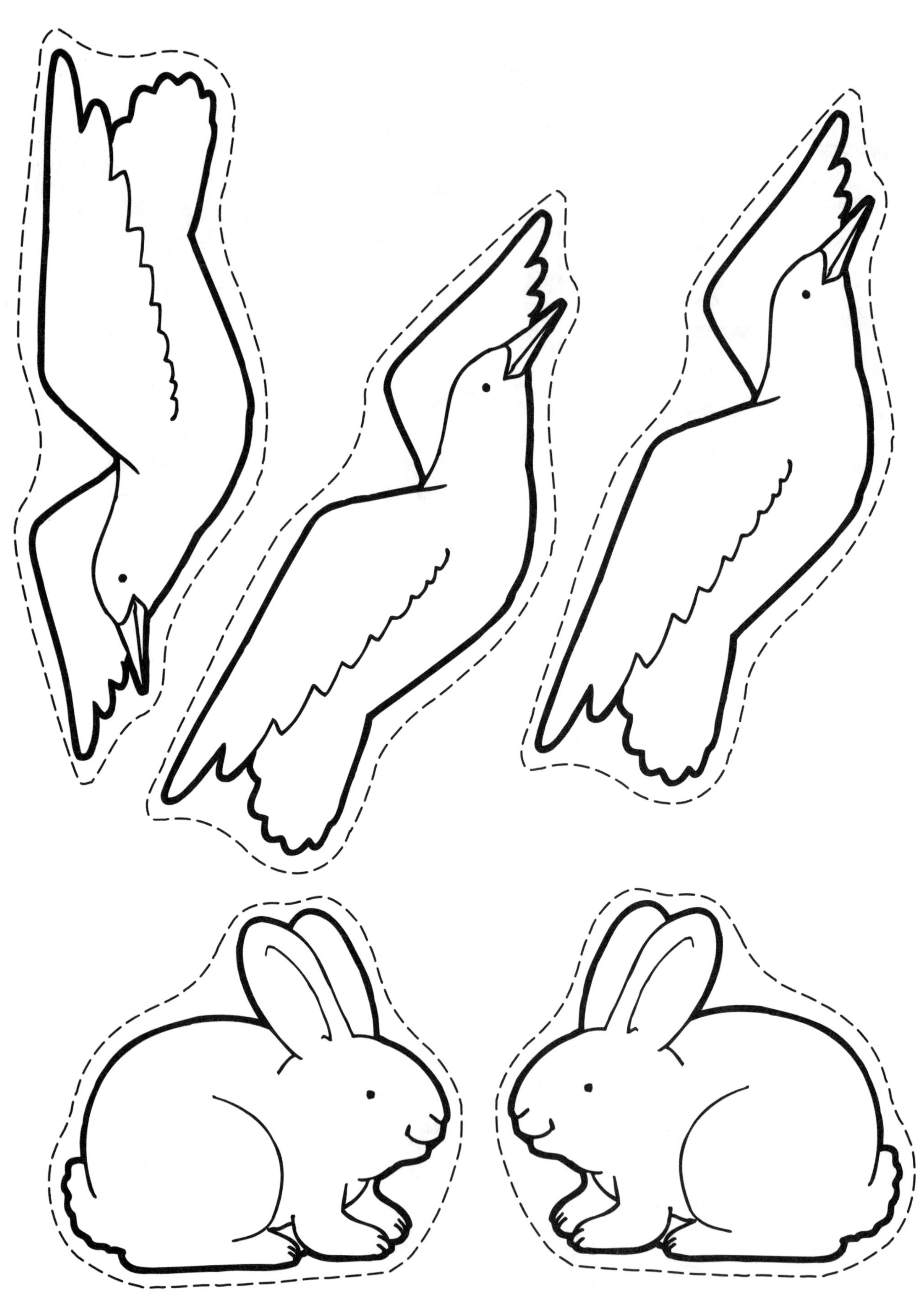

The Reproducibles

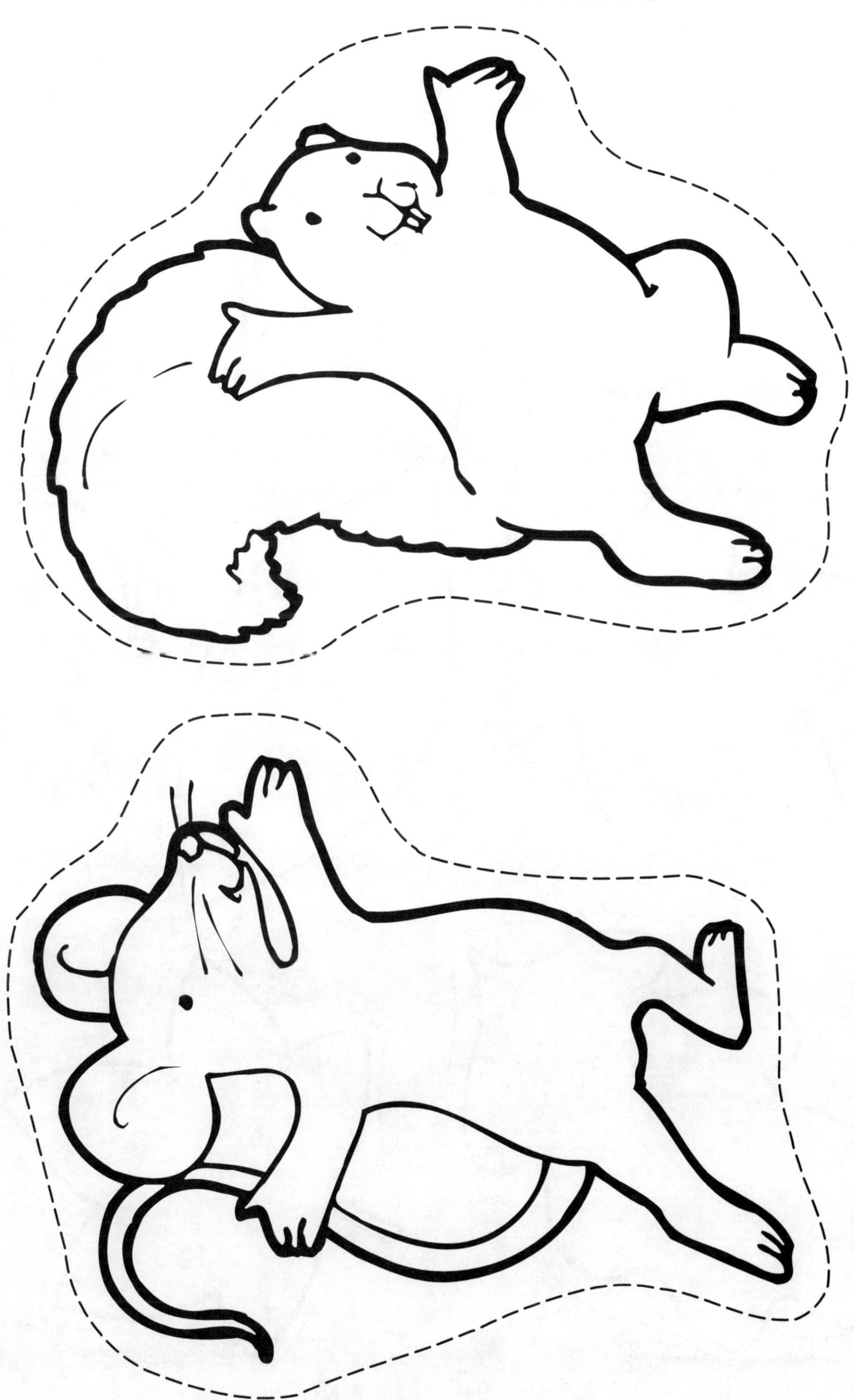

The Reproducibles

The Reproducibles

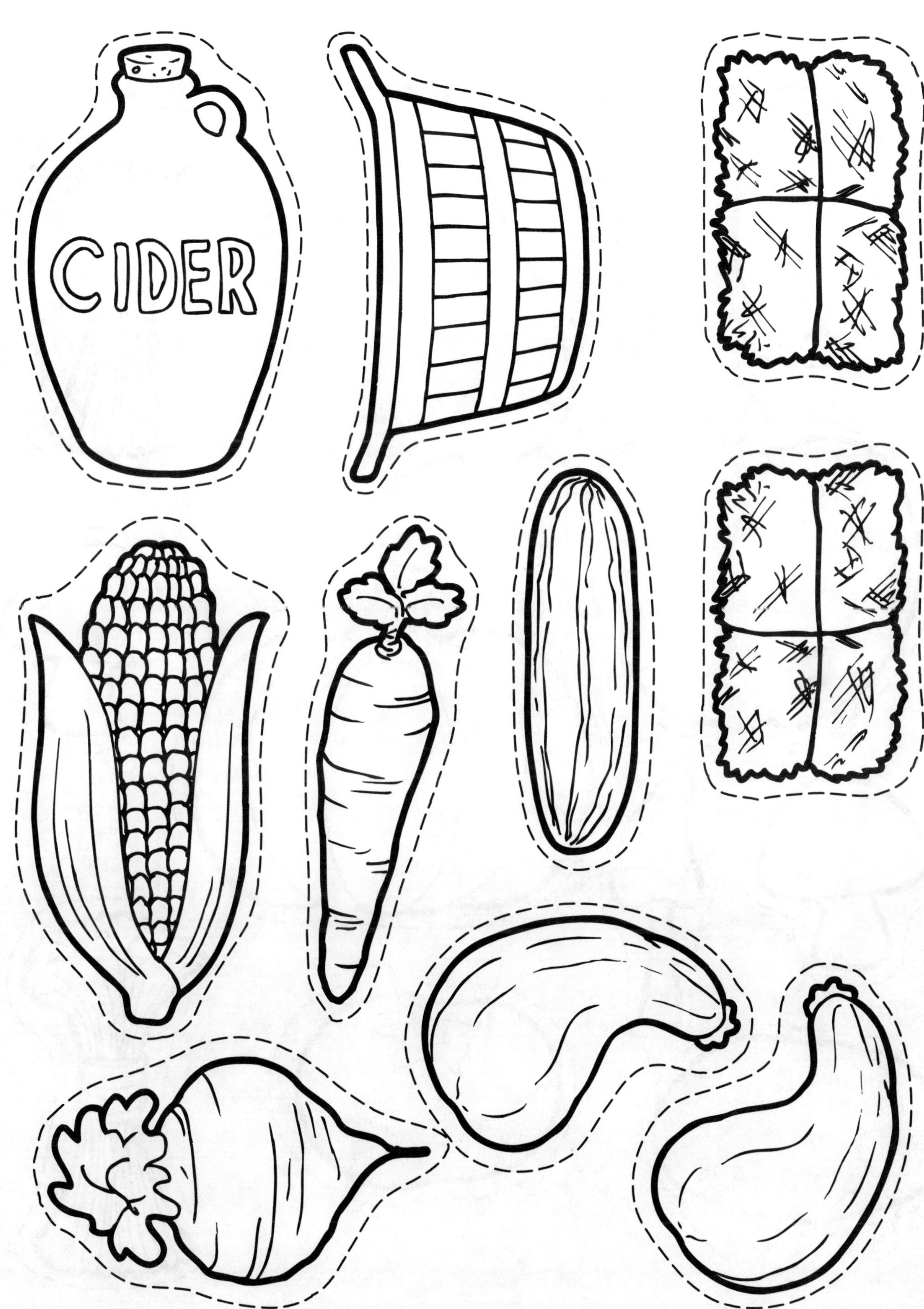

The Reproducibles

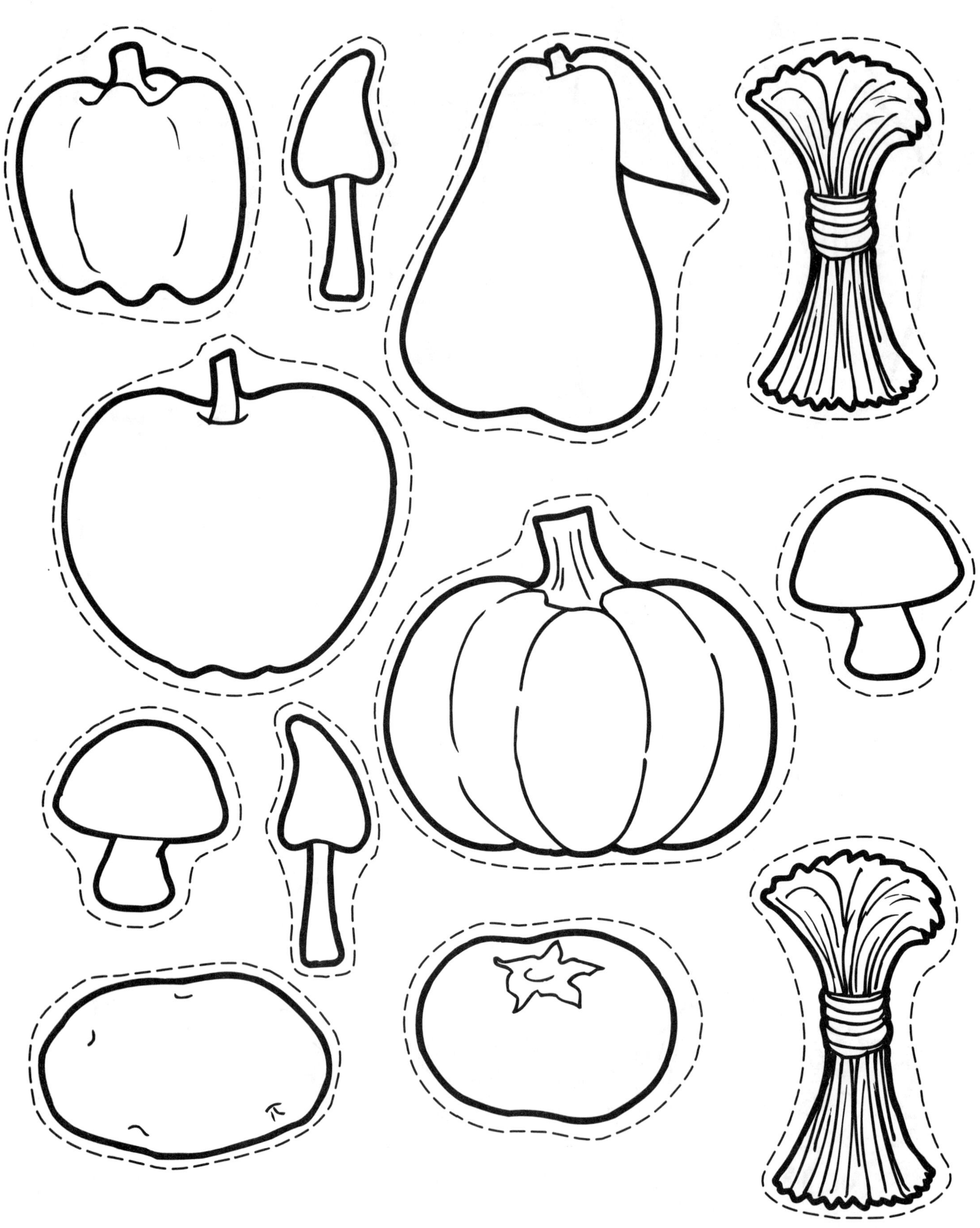

We're

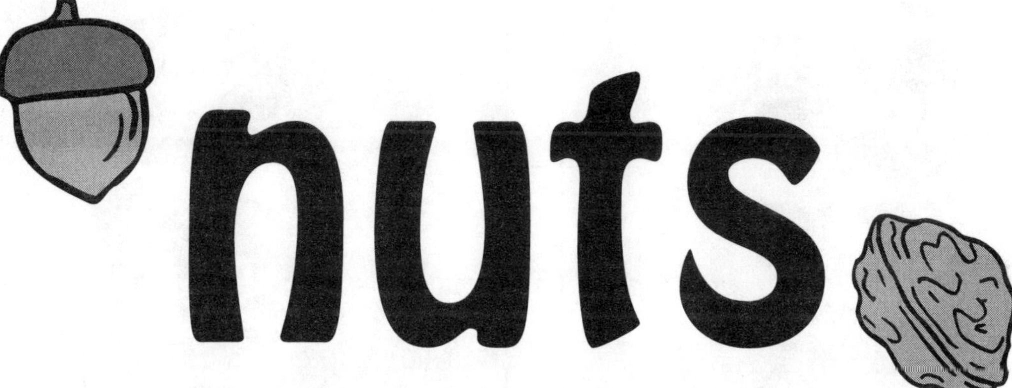

nuts

about

reading!

Autumn

Artifacts

Just "leaf" it to us!

The Reproducibles

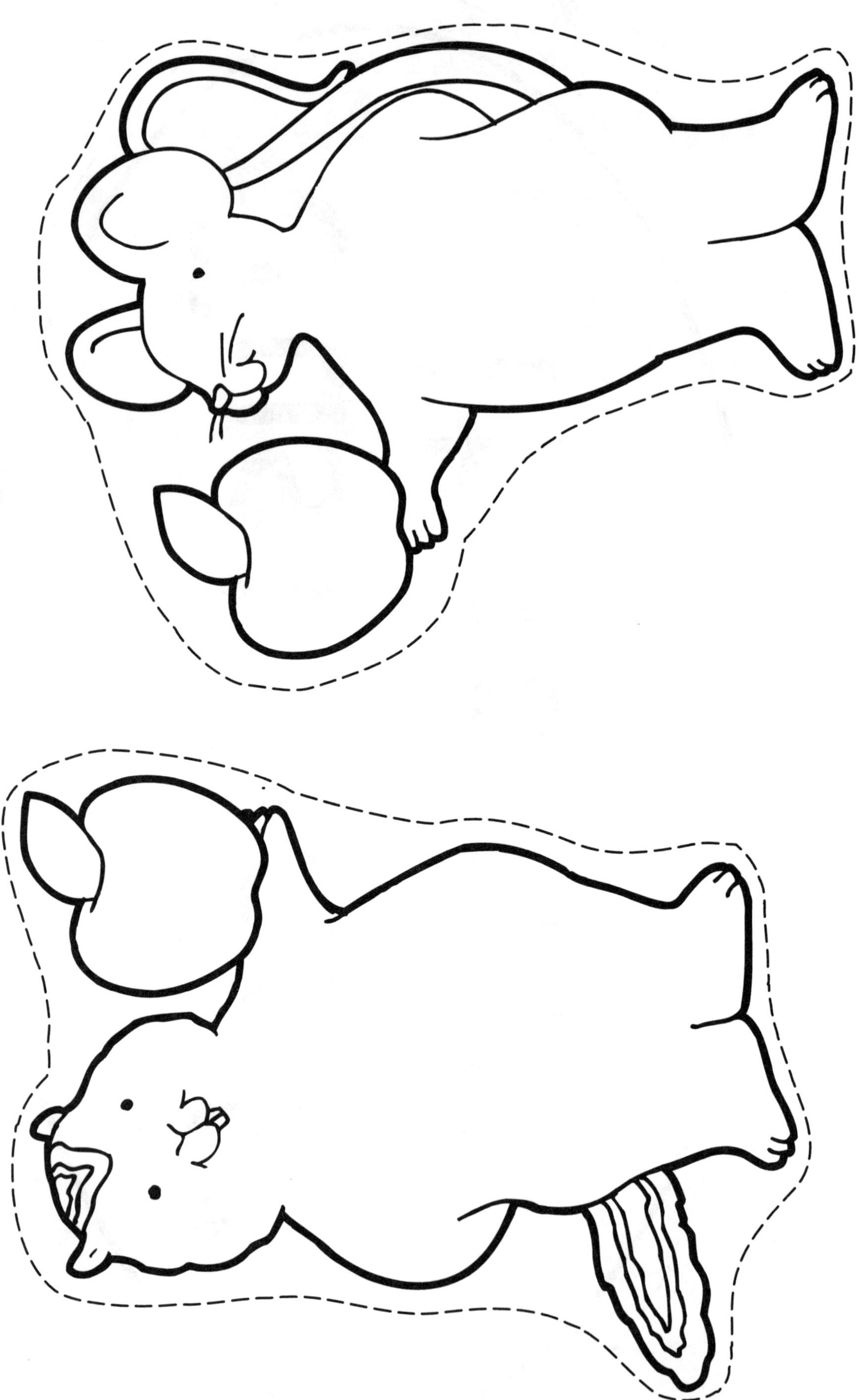

The Reproducibles

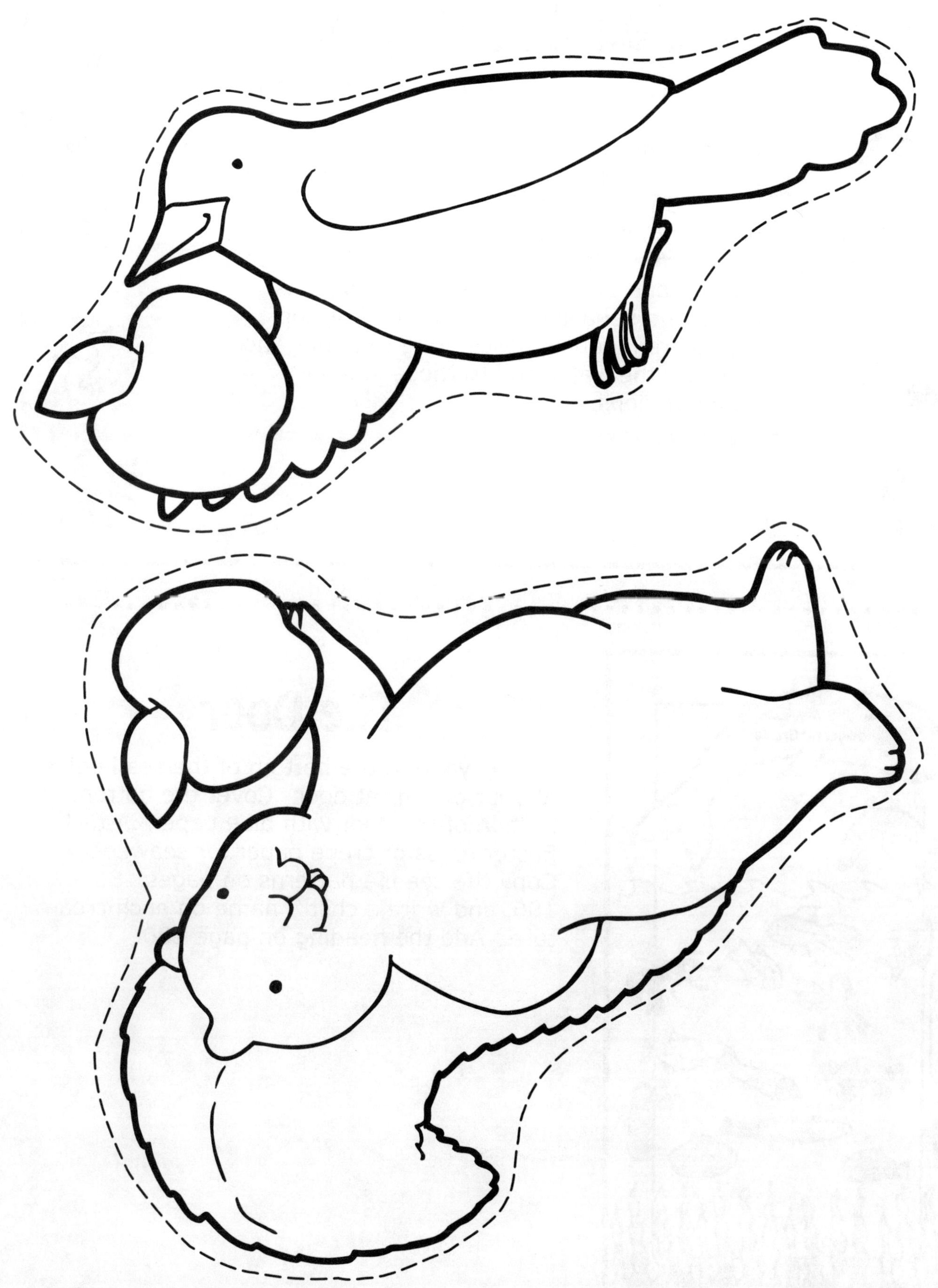

Sea Creatures

The seas are full of amazing life-forms, each adapted to its own habitat. In tidal pools at the edge of the shore, among coral reefs in tropical waters and down in the icy depths of the ocean, sea animals have developed ways of feeding, breeding and keeping themselves safe from predators. Sea life, with its clever adaptations and its wide variety of shapes, colors and behaviors, is an interesting topic for children, equally fascinating to those who live near the water and to those in land-locked regions.

The Door

Your voyage to the bottom of the sea begins at your own front door. Cover the bottom section of the door with blue paper. Attach Easter grass or crepe paper for seaweed. Copy the sea life patterns on pages 180-186, and write a child's name on each creature. Add the heading on page 180.

The Windows

Give your windows a wet, watery look with this simple trick. Purchase a roll of blue plastic food wrap, available in supermarkets. Cut two pieces of plastic wrap approximately the size of each pane you wish to decorate. (It is easier if you cut two pieces at the same time. Don't worry if the edges are jagged or if the wrap gets wrinkled.) Copy or trace some of the sea animals on pages 180-186 onto colored paper and cut them out. Stick one piece of plastic wrap on your window (no adhesive necessary). Place one or two animals on the plastic wrap. Put the second piece of wrap on top of the first. This will hold the animals in place.

The Ceiling

Look up and see a sea of sea creatures–you'll feel like you're under-water! Give each child two sheets of newspaper. Have children cut the two sheets at the same time into the shape of a sea animal. Staple the two sheets together around the edges, stopping about halfway to leave a wide opening. Gently stuff crumpled news-paper into the open-ing. Continue stapling around the edges. Paint the sea animal and add cut-paper details. Poke a hole through the top and attach a piece of string. Hang sea animals from your light fixture.

The Walls

The ocean is, indeed, full of life and this bulletin board will help children appreciate and classify the abundant treasures of the sea. Cover the lower portion of the board with sandpaper. Add a large paper rock. For water, cover the middle section with overlapping sheets of blue tissue paper. Use light blue paper for the sky. Ask children to contribute pictures of sea life, either drawings, magazine pictures or photos from a computer encyclopedia or the internet. Have them bring in shells, sea stars and other real items from the sea that they may have at home. Staple pictures to your bulletin board and use glue to attach shells and other three-dimensional objects. Add the heading on page 187. Label the creatures to help children categorize their findings.

The Walls

It's smooth sailing when you build a little camaraderie right from the start. Cover the top part of your board with light blue paper, the middle part with darker blue paper and the bottom part with tan paper. Have each child draw and cut out a self-portrait. Attach ships and text found on pages 188-189.

The Walls

Make a splash with this bulletin board designed to highlight children's work. Cover the lower part of the board with crumpled and twisted sheets of blue plastic wrap. Use cotton batting, pulled until thin and light, for clouds and whitecaps. Add art and heading on pages 190-191.

The Walls

Sharks are known for their razor-sharp teeth. But did you know that each tooth lasts only a few weeks? It falls out and another grows in its place, thus making the shark the perfect star of this "lost-a-tooth" display. You'll find the shark and the heading on page 192.

The Walls

Have fun with puns! Make up your own class rules to add to this display. Copy or trace the sea creatures on pages 180-186 and the heading on page 191. Add speech balloons.

The Desks

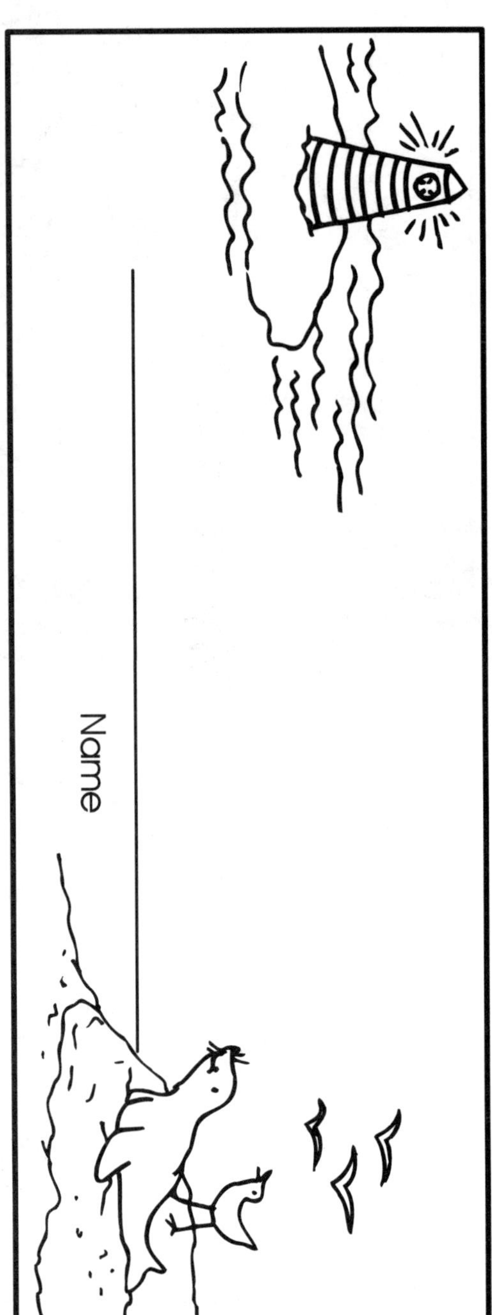

Folder Label: Glue a label on a file folder for each child. Use folders for in-class assignments and homework. Use the checklist to keep track of student work.

Desk Name Tag: Fold a 5½" x 7" (13.95 x 17.78 cm) piece of oaktag in half, lengthwise. Mount name tag on oaktag.

The Children

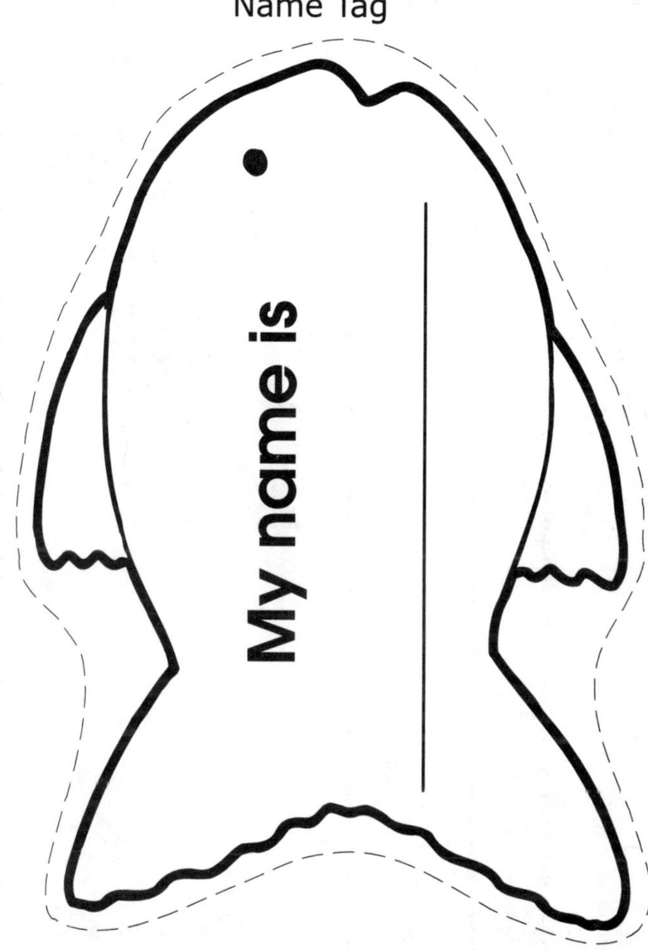

The Awards & Rewards

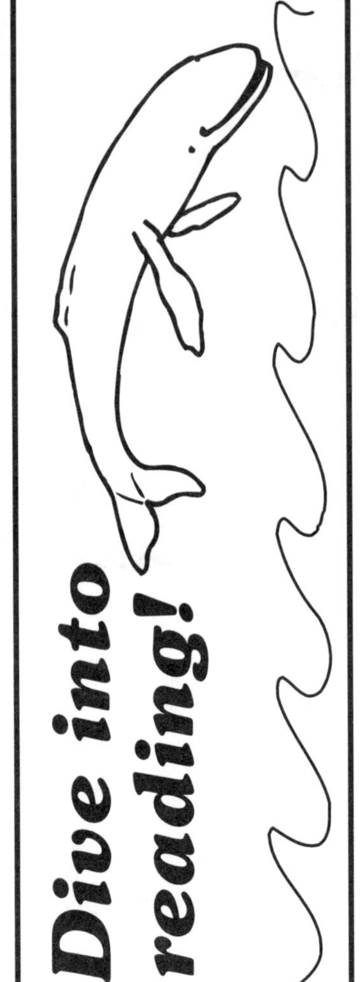

The Awards & Rewards

Award

To _______________________________

For a whale of a job in _______________________________

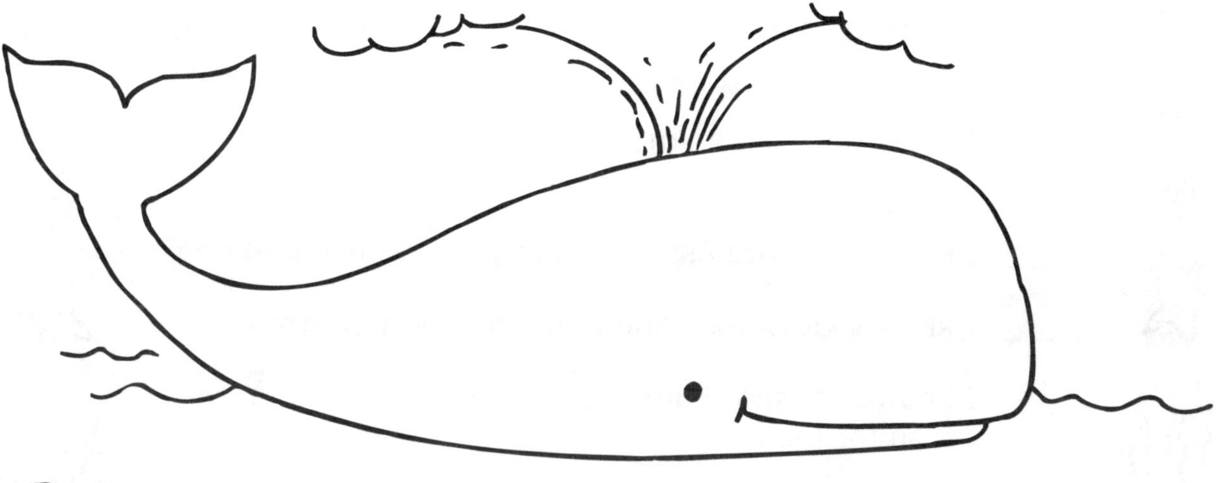

From _______________________________

We're all smiles! Here's why...

____

____

____

____

Signed _______________________________

Seal of Approval

Presented to

____

For _______________________________

By _______________________________

Name ________________________________

I Know! I Know!
All About Sea Creatures

_____ I know that the oceans are full of life.

_____ I know that there are many different habitats in the ocean.

_____ I know how sea animals have adapted to their habitats.

_____ I know that true fish have gills, backbones and fins.

_____ I know that whales and dolphins are mammals.

_____ I know that shore birds and animals depend on the ocean for food.

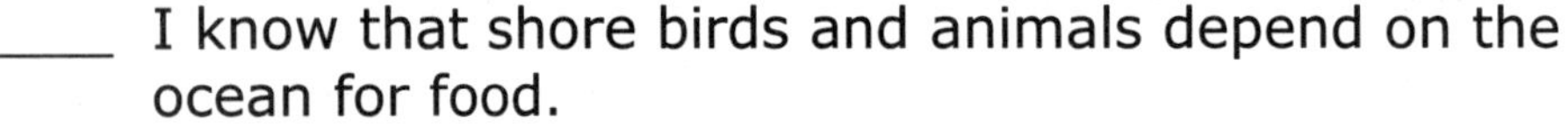

_____ I know that we need to protect sea animals from pollution and overfishing.

Draw an underwater picture below.

Name ___________________________

A Puzzle with a "Porpoise"

Use these words to fill in the answers to the puzzle.

ocean	sand	mammals	octopus
dolphin	whale	shark	seaweed
shell	birds	fish	

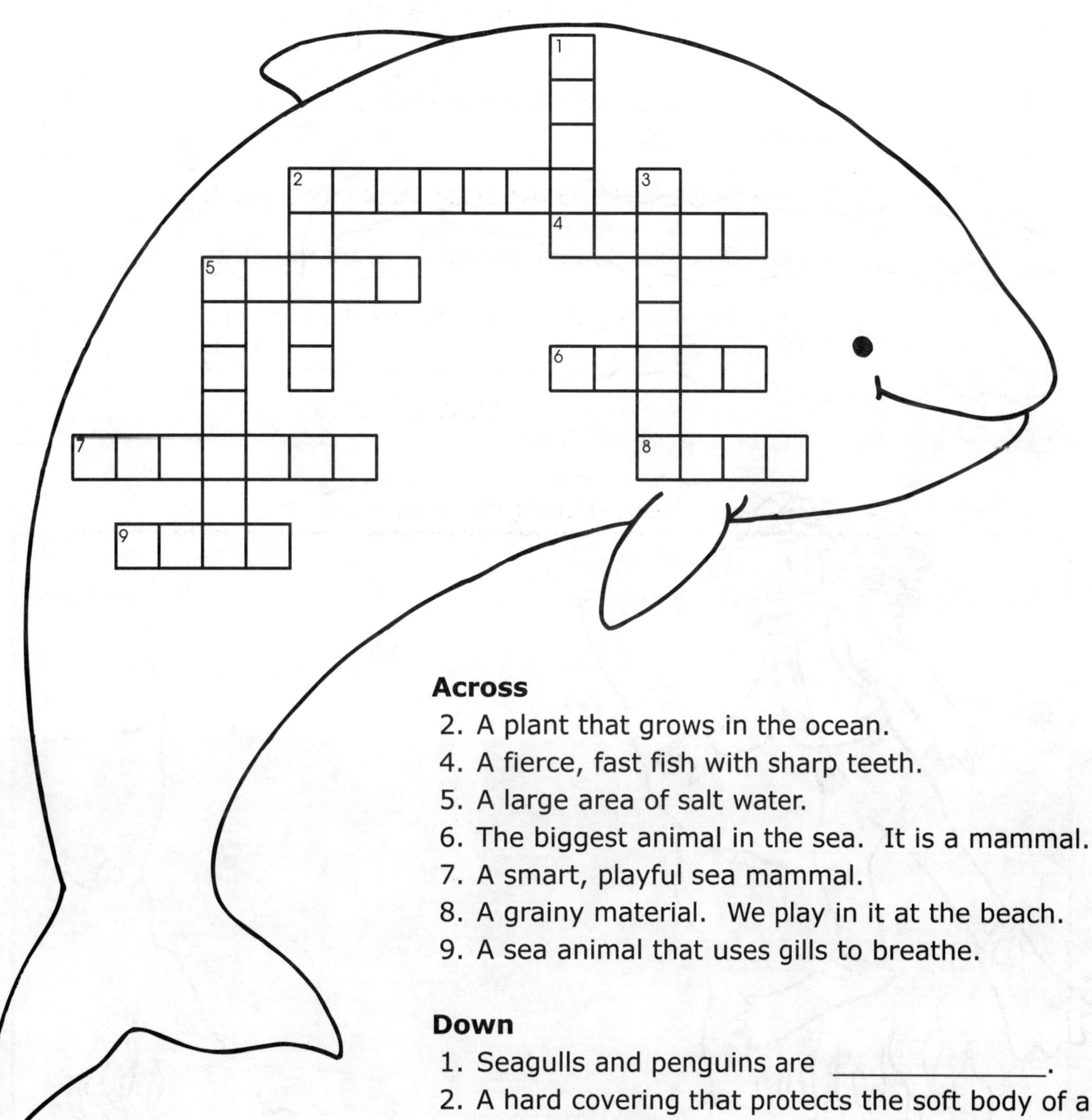

Across

2. A plant that grows in the ocean.
4. A fierce, fast fish with sharp teeth.
5. A large area of salt water.
6. The biggest animal in the sea. It is a mammal.
7. A smart, playful sea mammal.
8. A grainy material. We play in it at the beach.
9. A sea animal that uses gills to breathe.

Down

1. Seagulls and penguins are ______________.
2. A hard covering that protects the soft body of a clam or crab.
3. Seals and walruses are ______________.
5. A sea animal with eight arms called tentacles.

Take a Look at That!

What did the deep-sea explorer find at the bottom of the sea?
Draw something amazing in the underwater cave.

The Books & Media

Sea Creature Books

Into the A, B, Sea: An Ocean Alphabet
by Deborah Lee Rose and Steve Jenkins,
Scholastic, 2000.
This rhyming alphabet starring creatures of the
sea comes alive with astonishing cut-paper collages. A visual and informational treat for all ages.

Exploring the Deep Dark Sea
by Gail Gibbons, Little, Brown, 1999.
A look at the largely unexplored world beneath
the ocean's surface reveals dragon fish, viper
fish, sun stars and other incredible life-forms.

Baby Whale's Journey
by Jonathan London, Chronicle Books, 1999.
How a baby whale comes to know the ways of
the sea is captured with tenderness and drama.
Dynamic illustrations reveal the grace and mag-
nificence of endangered sperm whales.

Down, Down, Down in the Ocean
by Sandra Markle, Walker, 1999.
Readers explore descending ocean levels and
meet an array of animals, each uniquely adapted
to its particular depth in the Pacific Ocean.

Survival in the Sea
by Linda S. Lingemann,
Smithsonian Ocean Collection, 1999.
Describes a day and night in the life of a
hammerhead shark.

Follow That Fin
by Amy Samuels, Raintree Steck-Vaughn, 2000.
Follow two biologists as they study the behavior
of bottlenose dolphins in Shark Bay, Australia.

By the Seashore
by Tessa Paul, Crabtree, 1997.
Introduces seashore animals including the sand-
piper, sea turtle, crab, seal, sea otter, gray
whale and other creatures.

Destination Deep Sea
by Jonathan Grupper,
National Geographic, 2000.
Discover wonders of the sea–coral, sharks, box
jellyfish, octopus, squid, whales and more. The
spectacular photos and exciting, fact-filled story
make this a book to dive into!

How to Hide an Octopus
by Ruth Heller, Price Stern Sloan, 1992.
With full-color illustrations of sea creatures and
an informative, rhyming text, readers search for
exotic fish in the camouflage of the ocean.

Amazing Sea Creatures
by Andrew Brown, Crabtree, 1997.
An appealing presentation of seals, whales,
dolphins, salmon, octopuses and other sea creatures, their behaviors, defense mechanisms and
how they raise their young; with large realistic
illustrations.

Videos

The Little Mermaid
Disney, 1989.
Top-of-the-line Disney fun! With fabulous music
and sea creatures galore!

National Geographic's Really Wild Animals:
Deep Sea Dive, 1994.
Fun, funny and full of information and music,
this underwater tour combines animation with
live action footage. Part of an award-winning
series.

Web Sites

animalnetwork.com/
Click "fish" for profiles and
beautiful photographs of
aquarium denizens.

wh.whoi.edu/faq/
Fascinating fish facts in a Q&A format are presented by the Northeast Fisheries Science
Center. Do fish sleep? What is the world's
largest fish? How is the age of a fish deter-
mined? Suitable for primary
grades with adult assistance.

Row, Row, Row Your Boat

This cute and tasty little peach is such fun to make!
For each boat, you'll need:

lettuce leaves
1 canned peach half
2 small celery sticks
2 teddy bear graham cookies
handful of goldfish crackers
paper plate
optional: a toothpick, a small piece of fruit leather

- Arrange lettuce on paper plate.
- Place peach "boat" in the center.
- Add celery sticks for oars and teddy bears for sailors.
- Scatter goldfish on the lettuce.
- To make a sail, thread fruit leather on a toothpick and insert into peach.

The Deep Blue Sea Gelatin Cups

For a wonderful under-the-sea illusion, mix gummy fish candies into a batch of blue gelatin. Pour into clear plastic cups. When set, add whipped cream whitecaps.

The Clip Art

The Clip Art

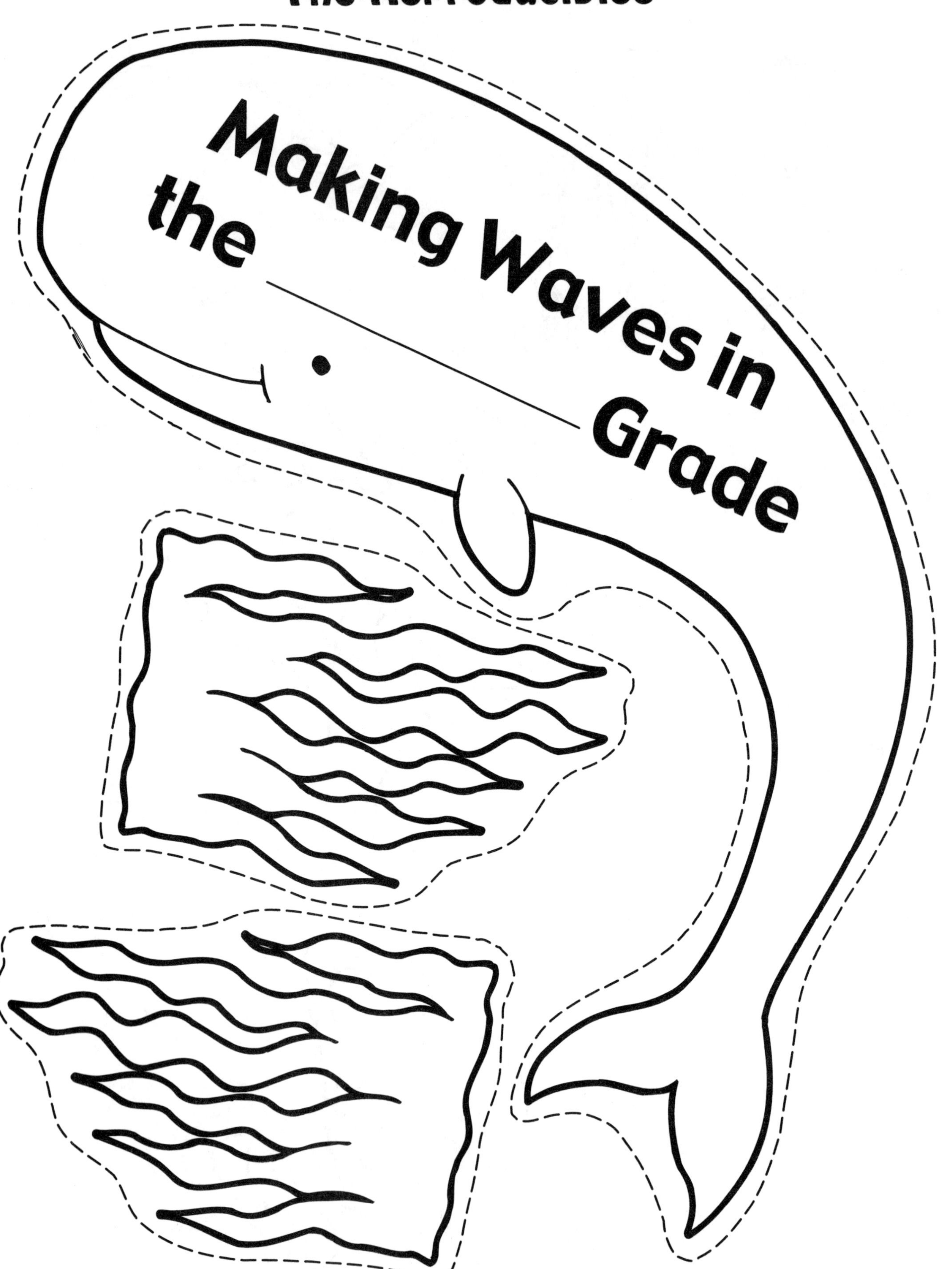

Making Waves in
the _______ Grade

The Reproducibles

The Reproducibles

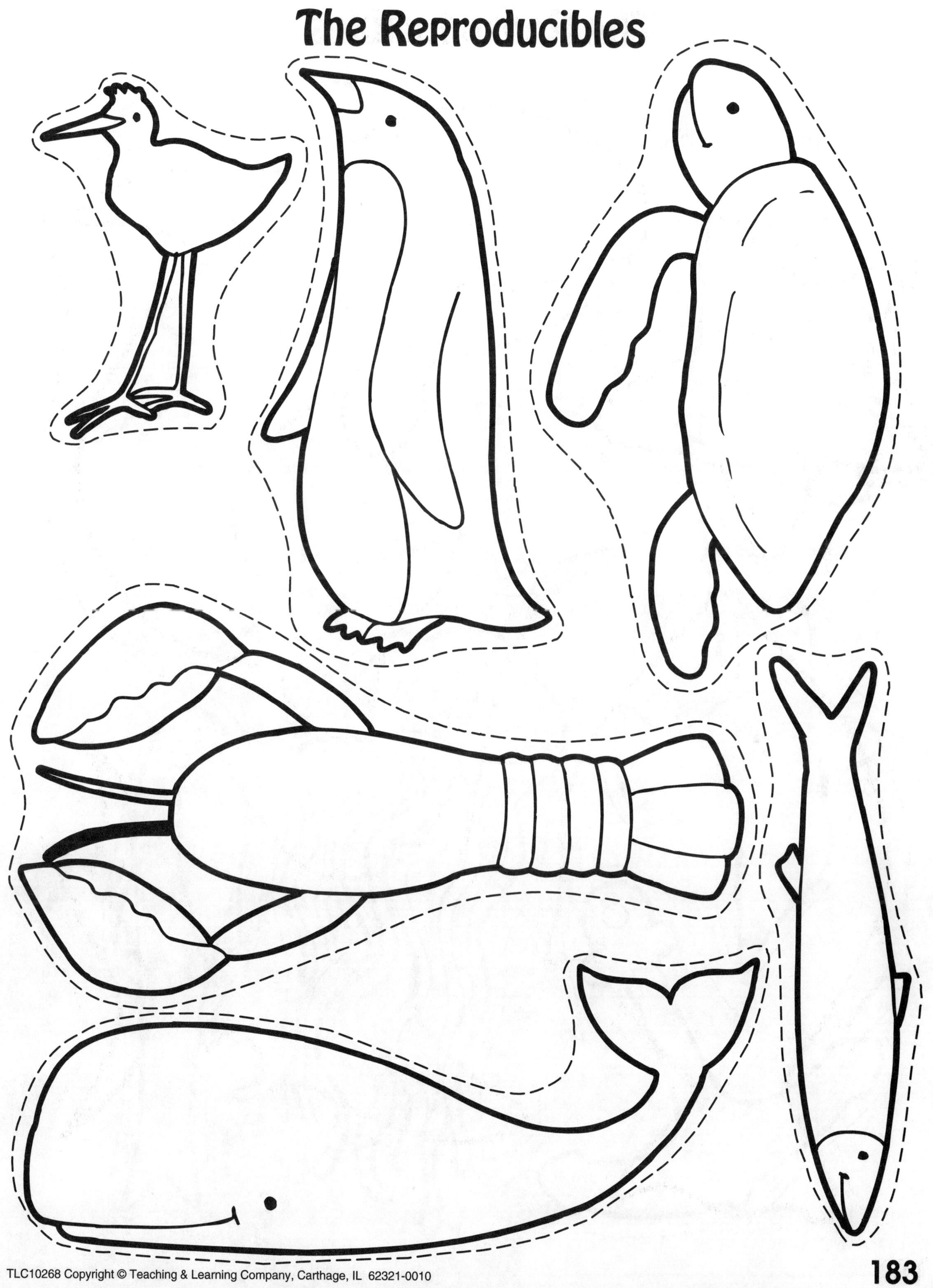

The Reproducibles

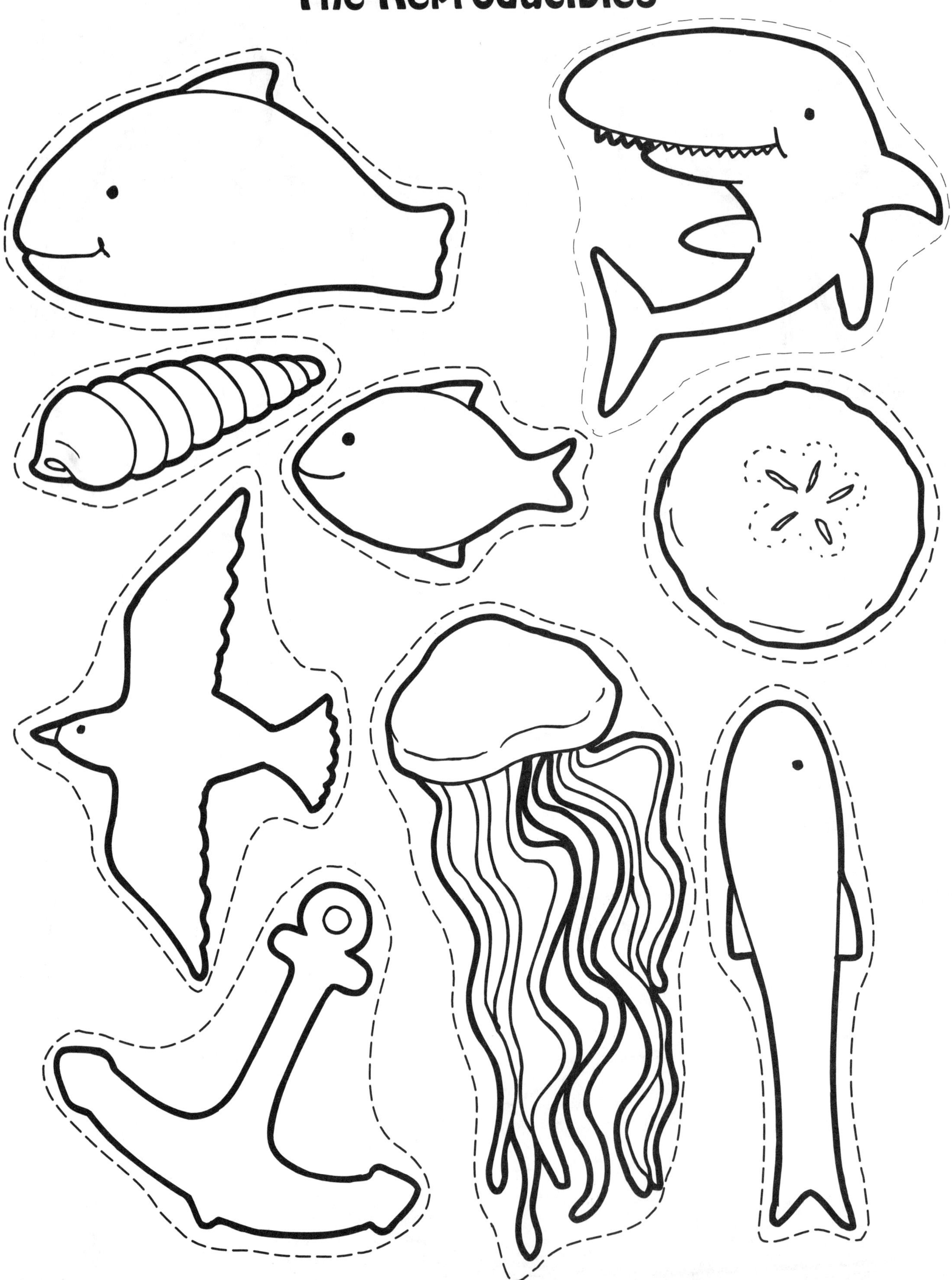

The Reproducibles

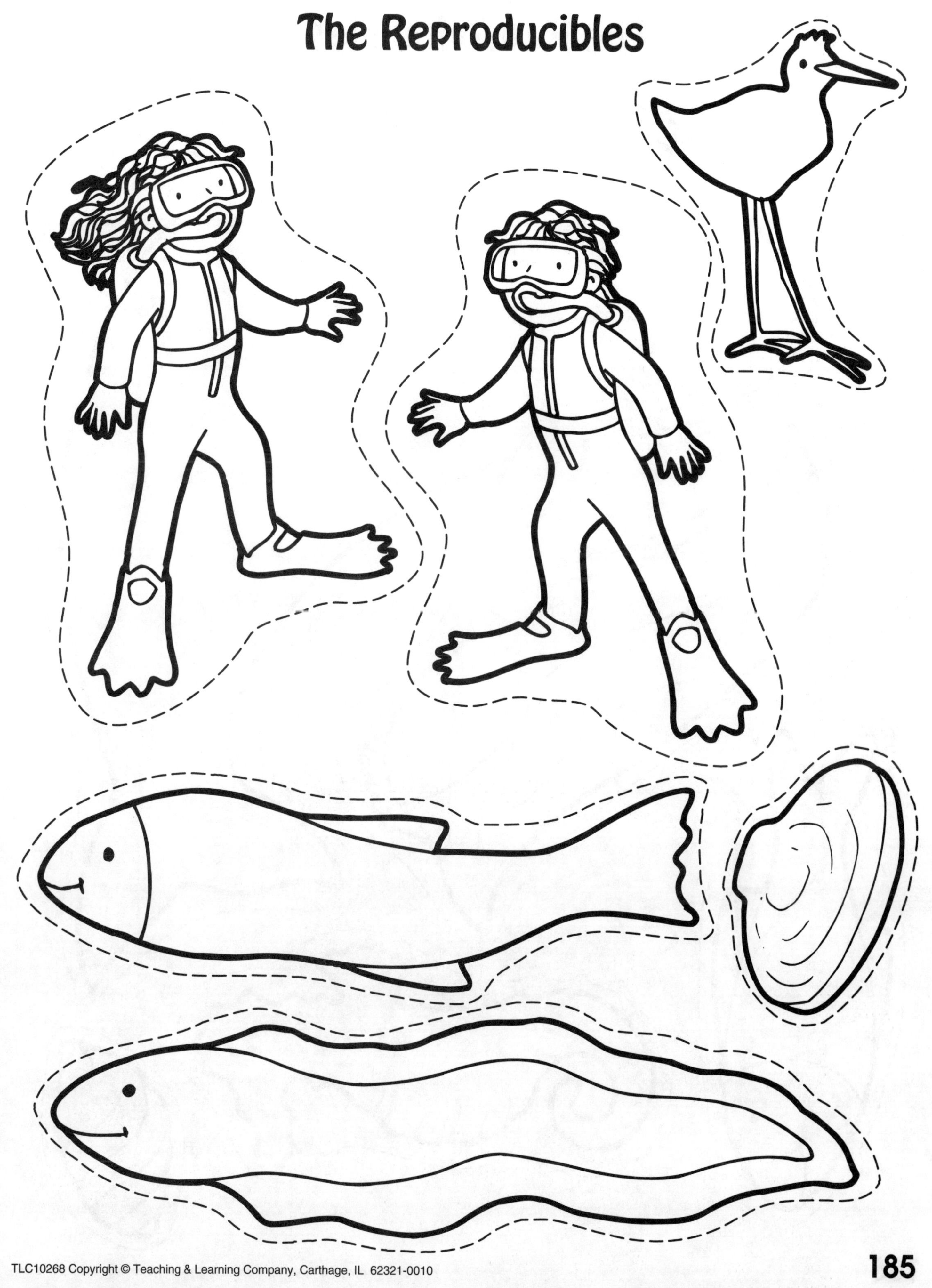

The Reproducibles

The

Ocean

Is Full

of Life

There are BIG ships,

And there are little ships,

But the best ship is FRIENDSHIP!

The Reproducibles

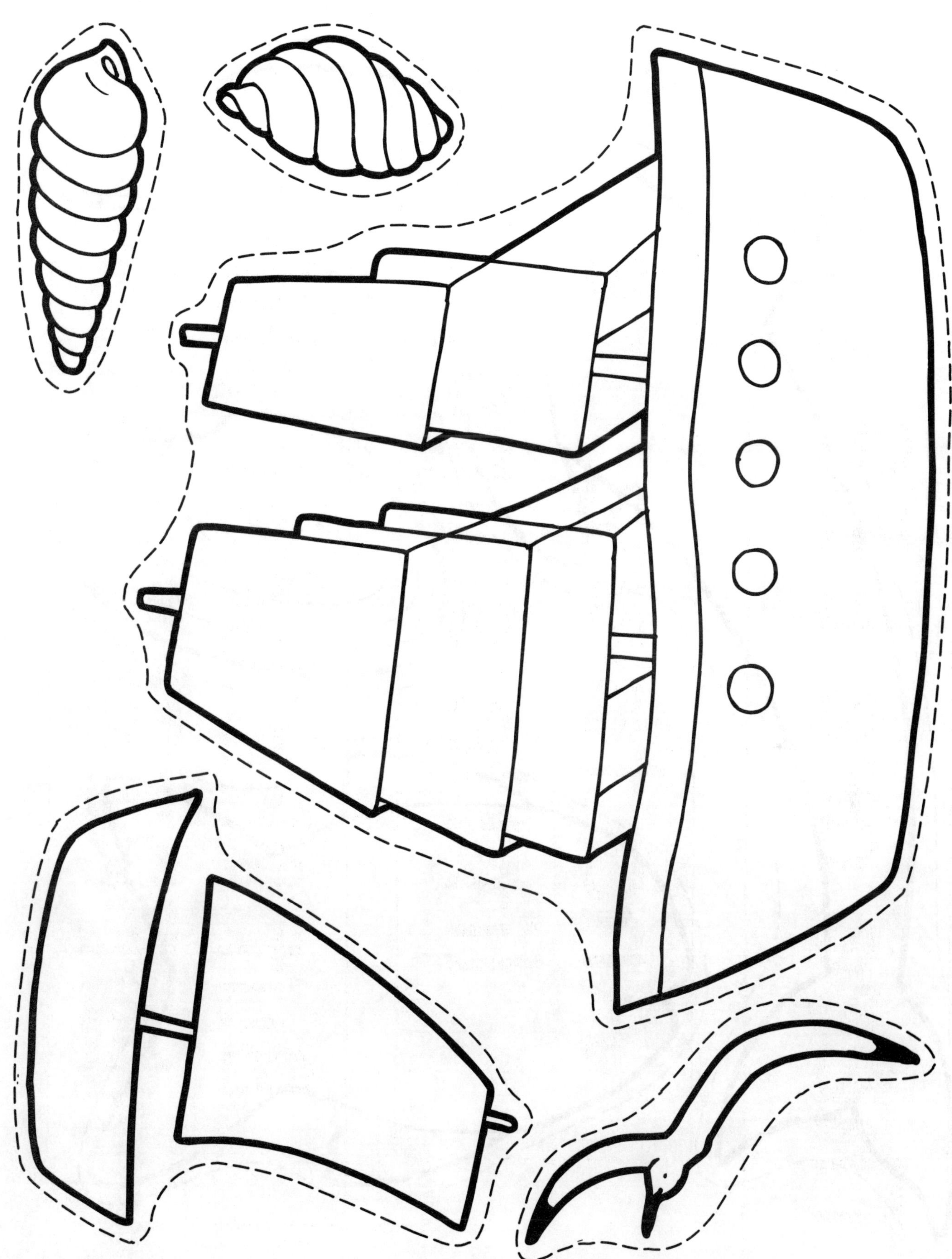

The Reproducibles

Learning by

Leaps and

Bounds

Class Rules!

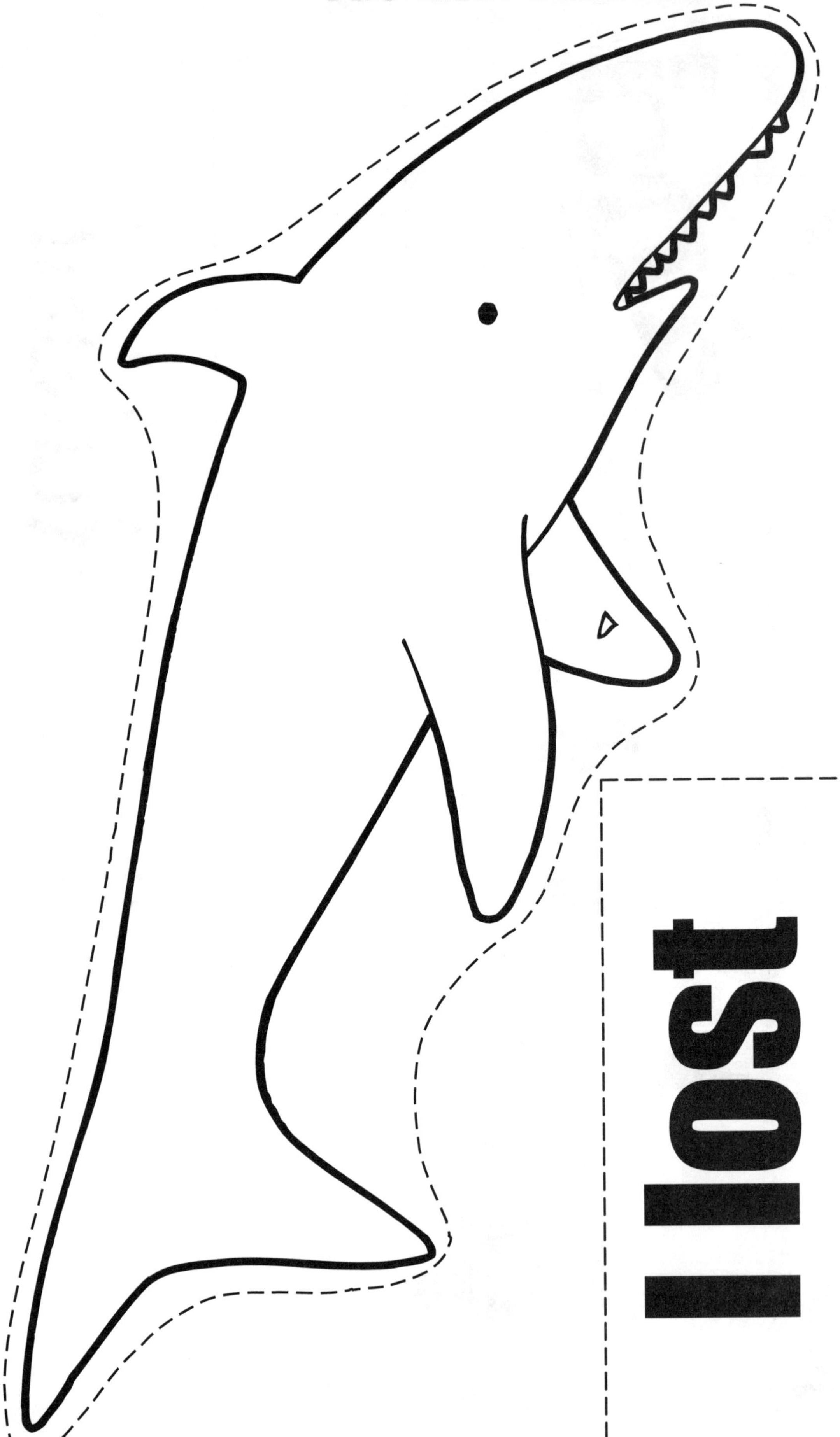

The Reproducibles

I lost a tooth!

Outer Space

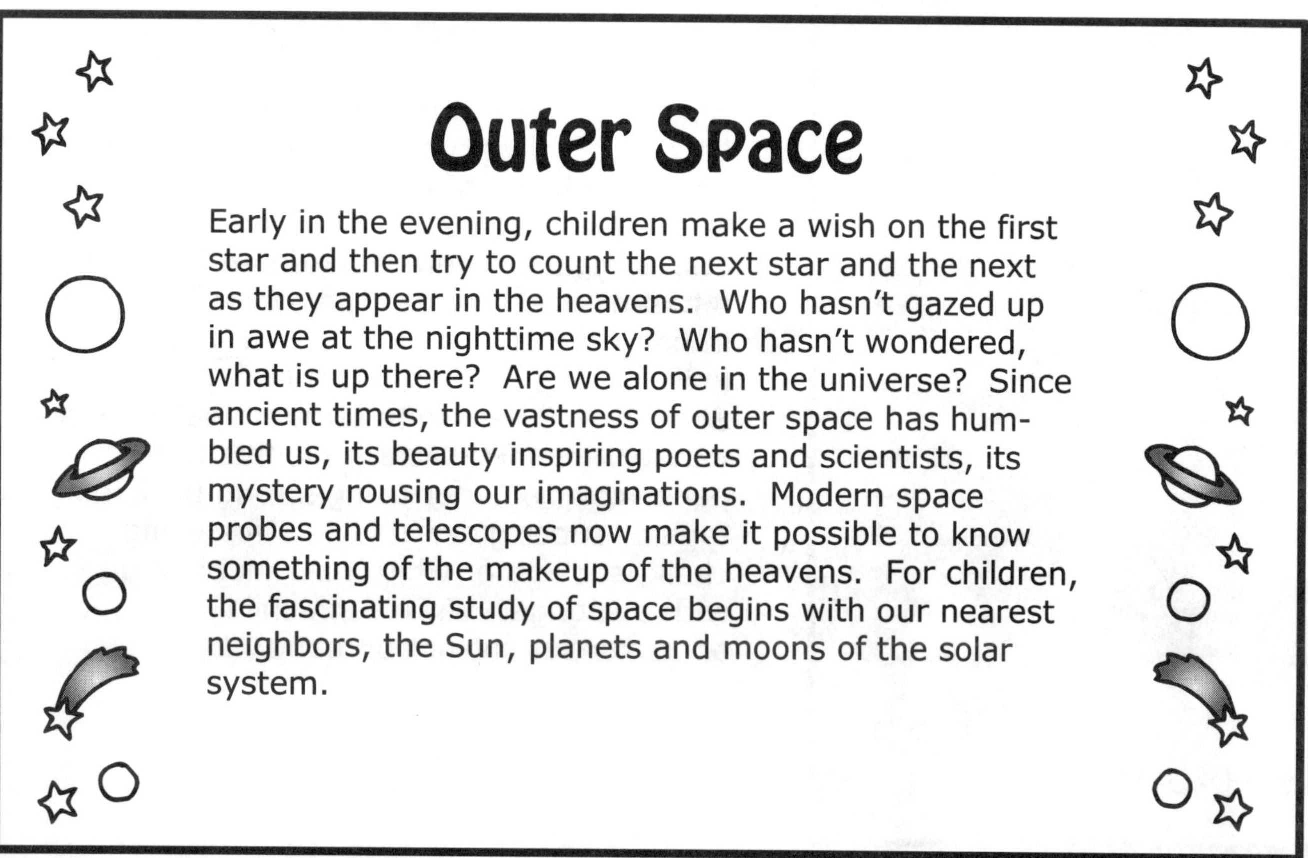

Early in the evening, children make a wish on the first star and then try to count the next star and the next as they appear in the heavens. Who hasn't gazed up in awe at the nighttime sky? Who hasn't wondered, what is up there? Are we alone in the universe? Since ancient times, the vastness of outer space has humbled us, its beauty inspiring poets and scientists, its mystery rousing our imaginations. Modern space probes and telescopes now make it possible to know something of the makeup of the heavens. For children, the fascinating study of space begins with our nearest neighbors, the Sun, planets and moons of the solar system.

The Hall

It's easy for even the littlest, not-yet-reading students to find their way to your classroom. Copy the heading on page 211 and the rocket pattern on page 212 to create a hallway sign. Copy the star and planet patterns on pages 217-218 to decorate the background. Position the sign near the school entrance. Make more copies of the rocket and tape them every few feet along the hall, from the hallway sign right up to your door. In your welcome-back-to-school letter, tell children to look for the rocket on the first day of school and follow it to the classroom.

The Door

Here's one way to make a dramatic entrance! Cover your door with black or dark blue bulletin board paper. Add the heading on page 213. To create the planets, purchase several Styrofoam™ balls in different sizes from a craft store. Cut them in half using a small saw or sharp kitchen knife. Using a brush or sponge, paint Styrofoam™ balls with tempera paints in a variety of colors. Attach planets to the paper-covered door using strong packaging tape or super glue. Create stars using chalk, stickers or white paint dabbed on with a sponge. Write each child's name on an astronaut cut-out on page 214.

The Ceiling

Don't let all that space above your head go to waste. Decorate it! To make out-of-this-world flying saucers, provide two aluminum pie plates or heavy-duty paper plates for each child. Poke a hole in the middle of one plate and attach a piece of string for hanging. Offer children a good selection of odds and ends for adorning their UFOs, including pipe cleaners, foil, sequins, paper clips, tinsel, glitter, beads, uncooked pasta, feathers, Styrofoam™ peanuts, crepe paper, bubble wrap, colored toothpicks, yarn and paint. Staple the two decorated plates together around the edges, and hang flying saucers from your ceiling or light fixture.

The Walls

Challenge your students to read, read, read with a reading race through outer space. Keep a tally of the number of books the class has read. Move the rocket ship from one planet to another when the children have read the number of books printed on each planet. When the class reaches the last planet, give each child one of the rewards on pages 199-200.

To make the display, cover your board with dark blue or black paper. Copy the heading on page 215 and the rocket on page 216. Cut a sun and planets out of colored paper and write a reading goal on each planet. Add children's drawings, book reports or photocopies of book covers if you wish.

• •

The Walls

Give each child an opportunity to shine with a place of honor on your bulletin board. Cover the board with black or dark blue paper. Cut large and small stars out of yellow paper or gold and silver foil. Copy some of the clip art on pages 209-210 and the heading on page 220. Mount a photo or self-portrait of the Star of the Week on the largest star. On smaller stars, mount drawings, photos or written lists of the child's family, friends, pets, favorite toys, books and activities. Give the Star of the Week special privileges (a class job of his or her choice, a seat at the front of the room) and an opportunity to bring in favorite items from home for show-and-tell.

The Walls

Cooperation and an art smock or old T-shirt are required when children work together to make this beautiful mural. Start with a large piece of mural paper or a solid light-colored sheet. Have children use broad, swirling brush strokes to cover the paper or sheet with varying shades of blue, purple and black paint. Let dry. Write *Reach for the Stars* across the top in white, silver or gold paint. On separate sheets of paper, have children draw, color and cut out planets, suns, stars, moons, astronauts, spaceships and aliens. Paste space art on the mural. (If you prefer, children may paint space motifs directly on the mural.) Hang your creation in the classroom, hallway, cafeteria, gym or library.

The Walls

Pride in one's achievements, big and small, is a step on the road to self-esteem. To make this display, cover the top part of your board with dark blue or black paper. On the lower part, attach crumpled butcher paper or brown paper bags to simulate the cratered surface of the Moon. Copy the heading on page 221, and the astronaut, rocket and the Earth on pages 222, 216 and 218 and color them in. Add star clip art or stickers. For a dramatic touch, attach a real flag to your display.

The Walls

What's happening in the world? What's new in your classroom? Here's a way to spread the word. Reproduce the bulletin board heading on page 223. Copy and color the Earth and satellite dish on page 224 and attach to the bulletin board.

The Desks

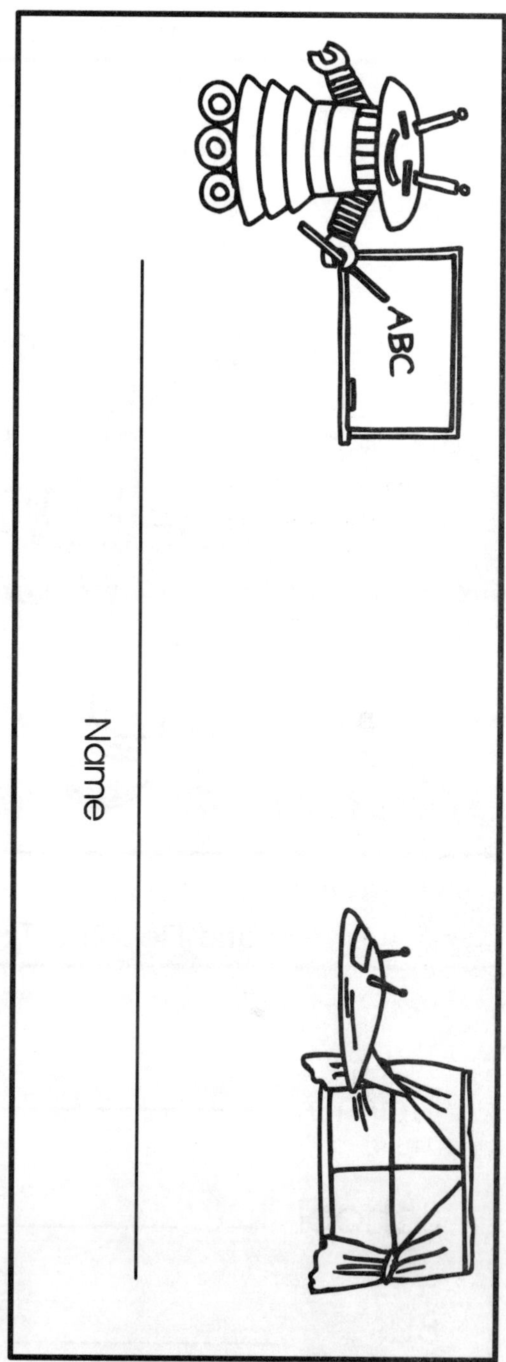

Folder Label: Glue a label on a file folder for each child. Use folders for in-class assignments and homework. Use the checklist to keep track of student work.

Desk Name Tag: Fold a 5 1/2" x 7" (13.95 x 17.78 cm) piece of oaktag in half, lengthwise. Mount name tag on oaktag.

The Children

My name is

____

Name _______________

School _______________

Bus _______________

____
Name

The Awards & Rewards

You're one in a million!

To ___________________

for special effort in math.

Signed ___________________

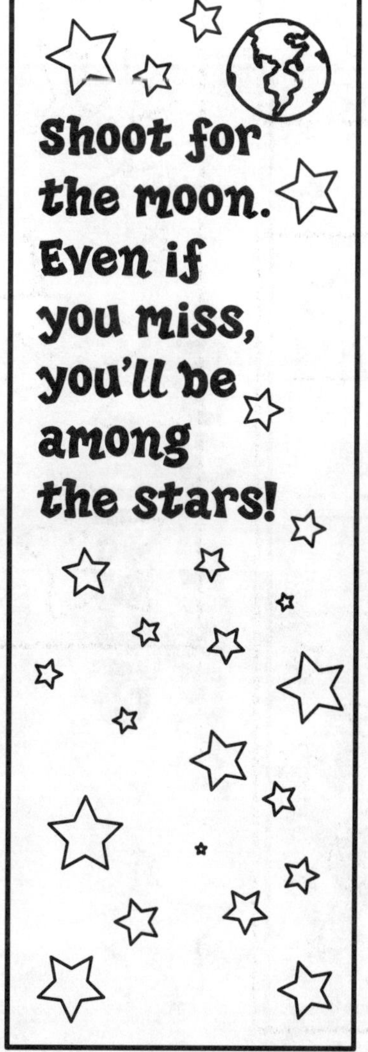

Reading is an adventure for the mind.

This book belongs to

____

The Awards & Rewards

Name _______________________

I Know! I Know!
All About Outer Space

_____ I know what the solar system is.

_____ I know the names of some of the planets.

_____ I know about stars and constellations.

_____ I know what the Sun is made of.

_____ I know what it is like on the Moon.

_____ I know what gravity is.

_____ I know how astronauts train to go up in space.

_____ I know about the space shuttle.

Draw an outer space picture below.

Pretend you are traveling in outer space. Write a postcard to your family telling about your amazing adventure. Draw a picture of something you have seen on your trip.

Greetings from Outer Space

Dear _________________________ ,

____

____

____

____

____

From _______________________

Stamp

Address

____

____

____

____

The Place We Call Space

Turn this page into a pocket-sized space dictionary. Have children:
Cut off this strip. Fold the page lengthwise on line A. Fold the page crosswise on line B.
Make sure the pages are in order. Illustrate each definition. Cut out a
cover and add the title: The Place We Call Space. Staple the cover to the booklet.

A

B

The **Moon** orbits around the Earth.
It is covered with craters and mountains.
There is no air, water or weather on the Moon.

4

The **solar system** is our neighborhood in space.
The Sun is the center of the solar system.
The nine planets orbit around the Sun.

1

The **Earth** is the third planet from the Sun.
It is the only planet that is known to have life.
It is our home.

3

The **Sun** is a giant ball of hot, glowing gases.
It provides light and heat to the Earth and the
other planets.

2

The Books & Media

Outer Space Books

The Planets
by Cynthia Pratt Nicholson, Kids Can Press, 1998.
Using NASA photographs, this well-done book includes fascinating facts, experiments, things to make and stories. Other books in the series include **The Moon; The Sun; The Earth; The Stars;** and **Comets, Asteroids and Meteorites.**

I Want to Be an Astronaut
by Stephanie Maze, Harcourt Brace, 1997.
Describes what it's like to be an astronaut, how astronauts train and other interesting space-related jobs.

Space Shuttle
by Mark Bergin, Franklin Watts, 1999.
Building the shuttle, lifting off, living in space, reentry and landing are some of the stimulating topics in this book.

The International Space Station
by Franklyn M. Branley, HarperCollins, 2000.
Part of the Let's-Read-And-Find-Out science series, this book tells about astronauts' lives aboard a space station, what might be discovered in space and other topics.

What the Moon Is Like
by Franklyn M. Branley, HarperCollins, 2000.
In this Let's-Read-And-Find-Out book, readers imagine the sights and experiences of a journey to the Moon.

The Planets in Our Solar System
by Franklyn M. Branley, HarperCollins, 2000.
This Let's-Read-And-Find-Out title describes the planets and includes directions for making models showing the relative size of the planets and their distance from the Sun.

The Starry Sky
by Patrick Moore, Copper Beech, 1999.
In a setting of splendid illustrations, readers tour the solar system and learn about stars, planets, comets, asteroids and meteors.

Stargazers
by Gail Gibbons, Holiday House, 1992.
Tells what stars are, why they twinkle, how constellations were named, how telescopes are used to study stars and other interesting facts.

1000 Facts About Space
by Pam Beasant, Kingfisher, 1992.
Every page of this stimulating book about galaxies, stars, planets, moon landings and modern astronomy is crammed with fascinating facts vividly presented with dozens of colorful illustrations.

The Magic School Bus in the Solar System
by Joanna Cole and Bruce Degen, Scholastic, 1992.
On an extraordinary field trip, Ms. Frizzle's class rockets into outer space. Pages are packed with nuggets of information and humor. A first-class introduction to the planets.

Web Sites

jpl.nasa.gov/
This colorful and attractive site offers photographs and news in large, easy-to-read type about the solar system, the Earth, the universe and current technology.

starchild.gsfc.nasa.gov
A learning center for young astronomers, this superb site offers information on the solar system and the universe on two levels, one for grades 2-3 and another for advanced third graders and older.

Alien Invaders Gelatin Mold

How do you vanquish an alien invader? You eat it!

lime gelatin (one box for four children)
small round glass bowls/dishes (one per child)
mini marshmallows
fruit pieces cut up for skewering (pineapple chunks, melon
  balls, grapes, apples, berries, etc.)
toothpicks or small wooden skewers
maraschino cherries
whipped cream
paper plates
plastic spoons

- Cook lime gelatin as directed.

- Pour gelatin into small glass bowls and allow to set firmly in
  the refrigerator.

- Once gelatin is set, remove from refrigerator, dip bowls
  quickly in warm water and unmold onto plates with the
  rounded side facing up.

- Make alien antennas by threading fruit and mini marshmallows onto toothpicks or skewers. Use maraschino cherries
  for eyes.

- Create a border around the base of the mold with whipped
  cream and fruit.

- Have children make up names for their aliens and then zap!
  All gone!

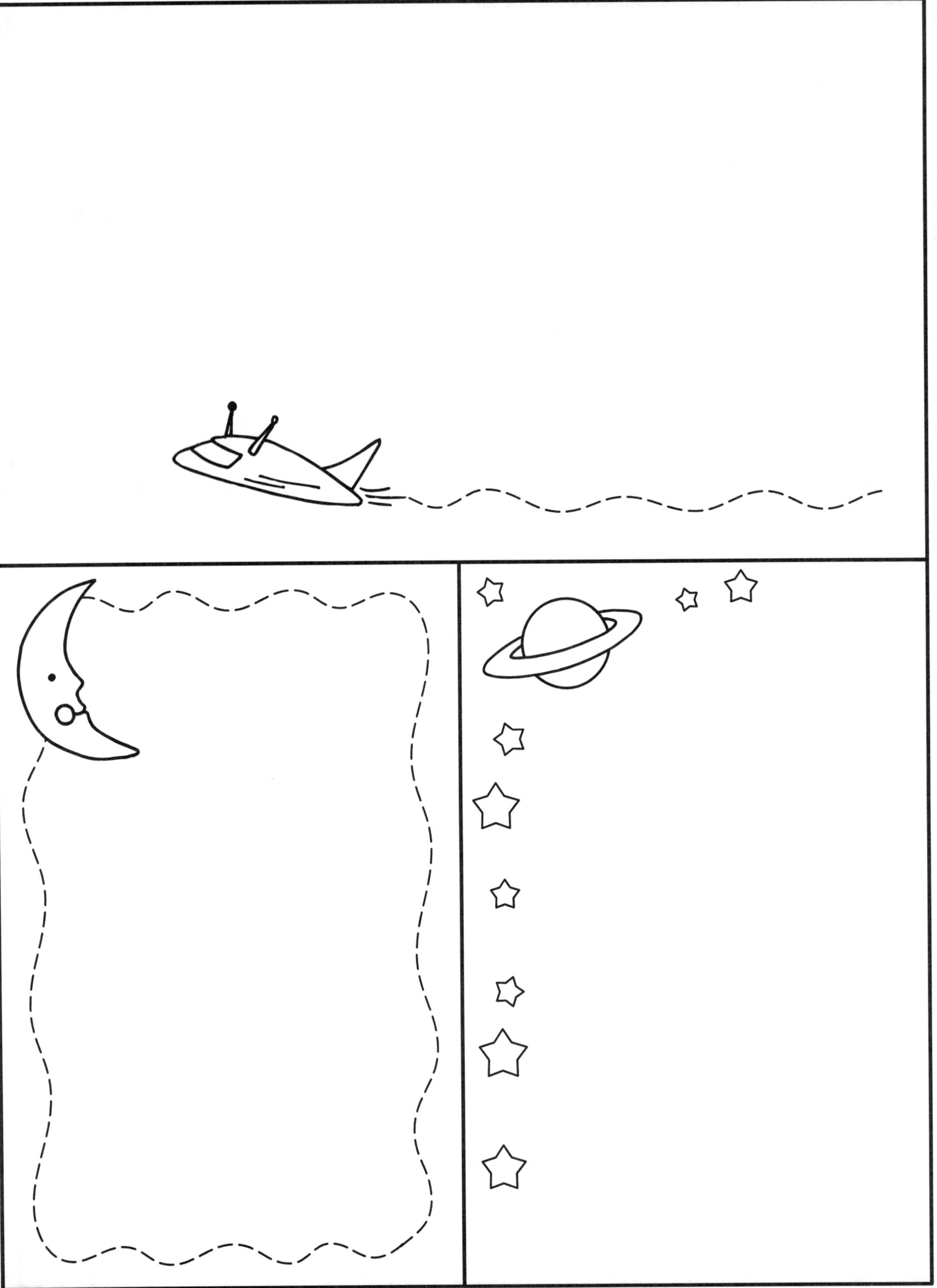

The Clip Art

The Clip Art

The Reproducibles

Follow the

rocket

to Room ______

The Reproducibles

Welcome
to Our
World

The Reproducibles

Space Race
Blast Off with
Books!

The Reproducibles

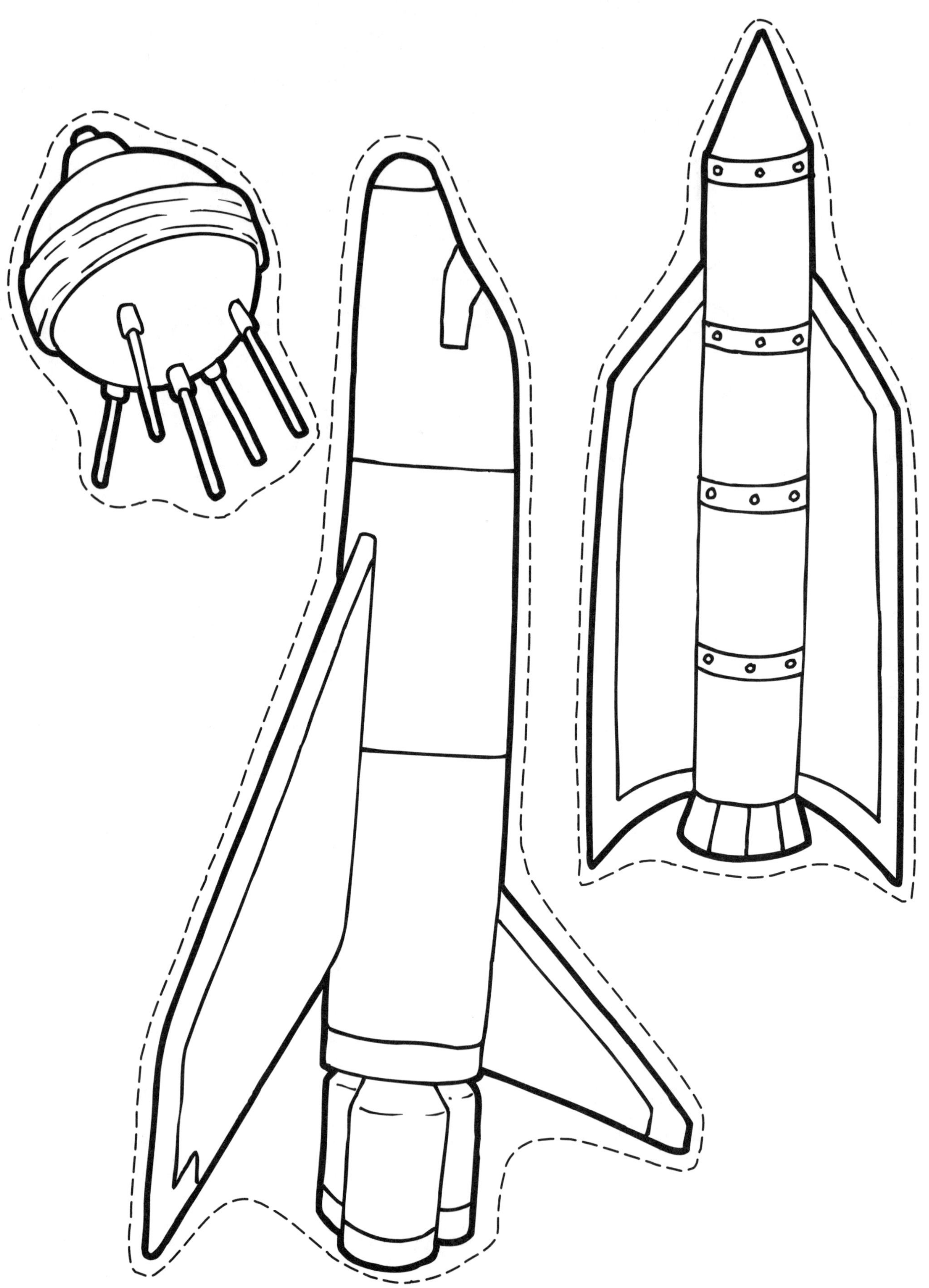

The Reproducibles

The Reproducibles

The Reproducibles

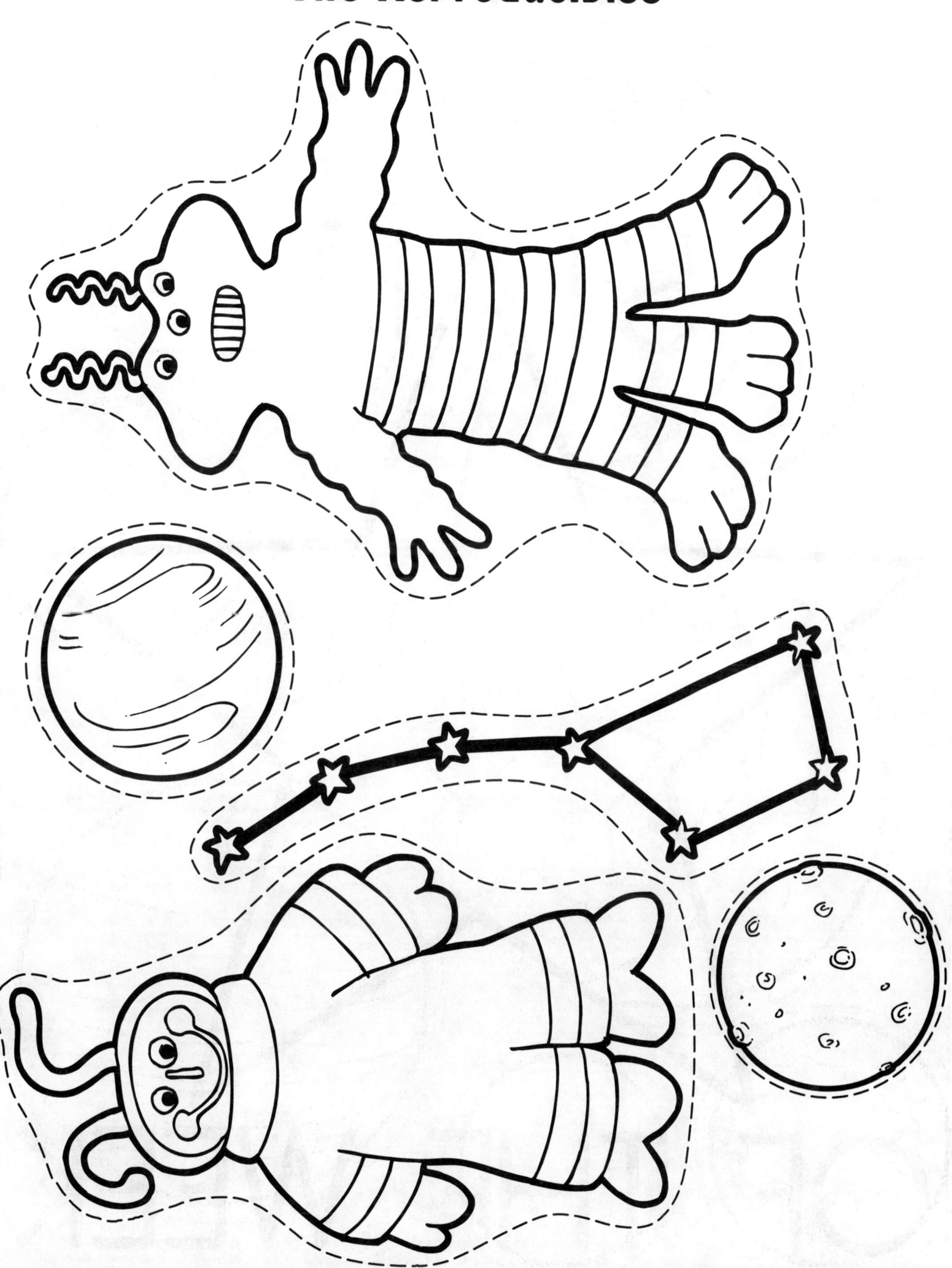

STAR
OF THE WEEK

I did it!

The Reproducibles

222

News and Views from Planet Earth

The Reproducibles

Classic Tales

A celebration of books and reading is a theme that runs throughout the chapters of this back-to-school book. In this unit, our love of books takes center stage with displays and activities based on four classic tales–*The Wonderful Wizard of Oz*, *Alice's Adventures in Wonderland*, *Peter Pan* and *The Adventures of Pinocchio*. The four tales have much in common. Each is a journey into a realm of fantasy. Each has a main character who learns an important life lesson by the end of the story. And each is told in rich, colorful, playful language, perfect for reading aloud or for competent third grade readers to try on their own. If, like most children, your students know these stories only through the movies, introduce them to one or all of the books, preferably in the original, full-length version. You may decide to give children a taste of the four books by reading aloud a chapter from each one. Then let them choose which book they want you to read in its entirety, a few pages or a chapter a day. Enjoy!

The Hall

It's fun to start the school year with a trip down the yellow brick road. Copy the heading on page 245 and the characters on page 243 to create this hallway sign. Post the sign in the hall near the school entrance. Create a yellow brick road by taping sheets of yellow paper every few feet along the wall, from the sign all the way to your door. (You may want to decorate the yellow paper with a brick pattern.) In your back-to-school letter, be sure to tell the children to follow the yellow brick road when they enter the building on the first day of school.

The Door

Your door's colorful storybook parade tells one and all, "This is a place for fun and learning." Cut stepping-stones out of yellow paper and write a child's name on each one. Create a rainbow and tree out of construction paper. Copy the book characters on pages 243-244 and 247-251, color them in and add them to your display.

The Walls

Are your students hooked on books . . . or math . . . or science? You can adapt this bulletin board to showcase work in any subject. You'll find patterns for the characters on pages 247-248 and the heading on page 246.

The Walls

Celebrate the excellent work of your "mad adders." Cut a simple table out of construction paper. Cut teacups out of colorful wrapping paper. To create card characters, punch holes in the sides of playing cards and insert pipe cleaners for arms and legs. Glue on a paper head, and if you'd like, yarn for hair. Copy the storybook characters on pages 249-250 and the heading on page 249, and attach them to the board.

The Walls

Pinocchio learned his lesson the hard way, by getting into trouble at every turn. This bulletin board reminds children to behave responsibly. Have students draw a large picture of Pinocchio on oaktag and cut it out. Then have them cut off the arms and legs. Reattach arms and legs with brad fasteners. Tape a piece of string to each foot and hand. Then tape the ends of the four strings to a strip of oaktag. Mount puppets on your bulletin board along with the heading on page 252. Add the safety rules that apply to your students.

The Walls

This beautiful frieze, a collaborative effort, puts children in touch with literature. Have students illustrate a character or scene from a favorite book and add a sentence or two describing it. Copy page 253 and mount it above your chalkboard. Next to it, hang children's pictures, side-by-side, encircling your room. At the end, mount a copy of page 254.

The Walls

Help is on the way with this charming "chore board." Copy the characters on pages 255-256. Cut a slit in the top of each book. Write children's names on oaktag bookmarks and insert bookmarks into books when assigning chores. Top off your display with the heading on page 252.

The Desks

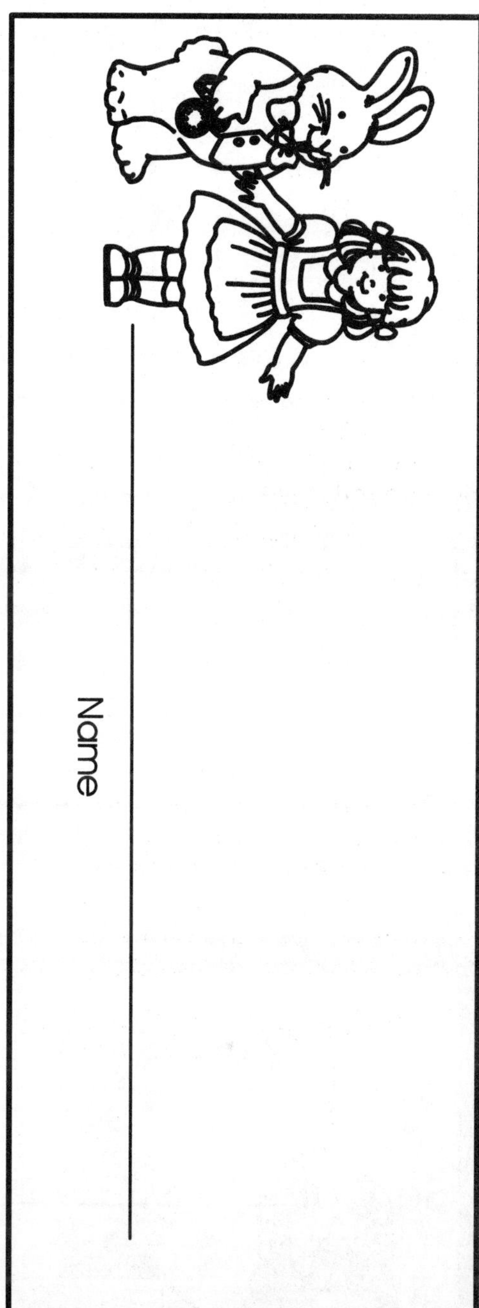

Folder Label: Glue a label on a file folder for each child. Use folders for in-class assignments and homework. Use the checklist to keep track of student work.

Desk Name Tag: Fold a 5½" x 7" (13.95 x 17.78 cm) piece of oaktag in half, lengthwise. Mount name tag on oaktag.

The Children

Name

Bus and Field Trip Tag

Name ___________

School ___________

Bus ___________

The Awards & Rewards

The Awards & Rewards

To _______________________

From _______________________

You're flying high!

Here's why _______________________

____

____

This

Acts of Kindness Award

Is for

____

"Because of the wonderful things you do!"

From _______________________

Special Effort Award

Presented to

____

For _______________________

From _______________________

No strings attached!

I Know! I Know!
All About Classic Tales

_____ I know the story of *Peter Pan*.

_____ I know the story of *The Wonderful Wizard of Oz*.

_____ I know the story of *Alice's Adventures in Wonderland*.

_____ I know the story of *The Adventures of Pinocchio*.

_____ I know where to find a good book.

_____ I know it is important to read every day.

Draw a picture of a book character below.

Alice's A-Mazing Adventure

Use your pencil to help Alice find her way home.

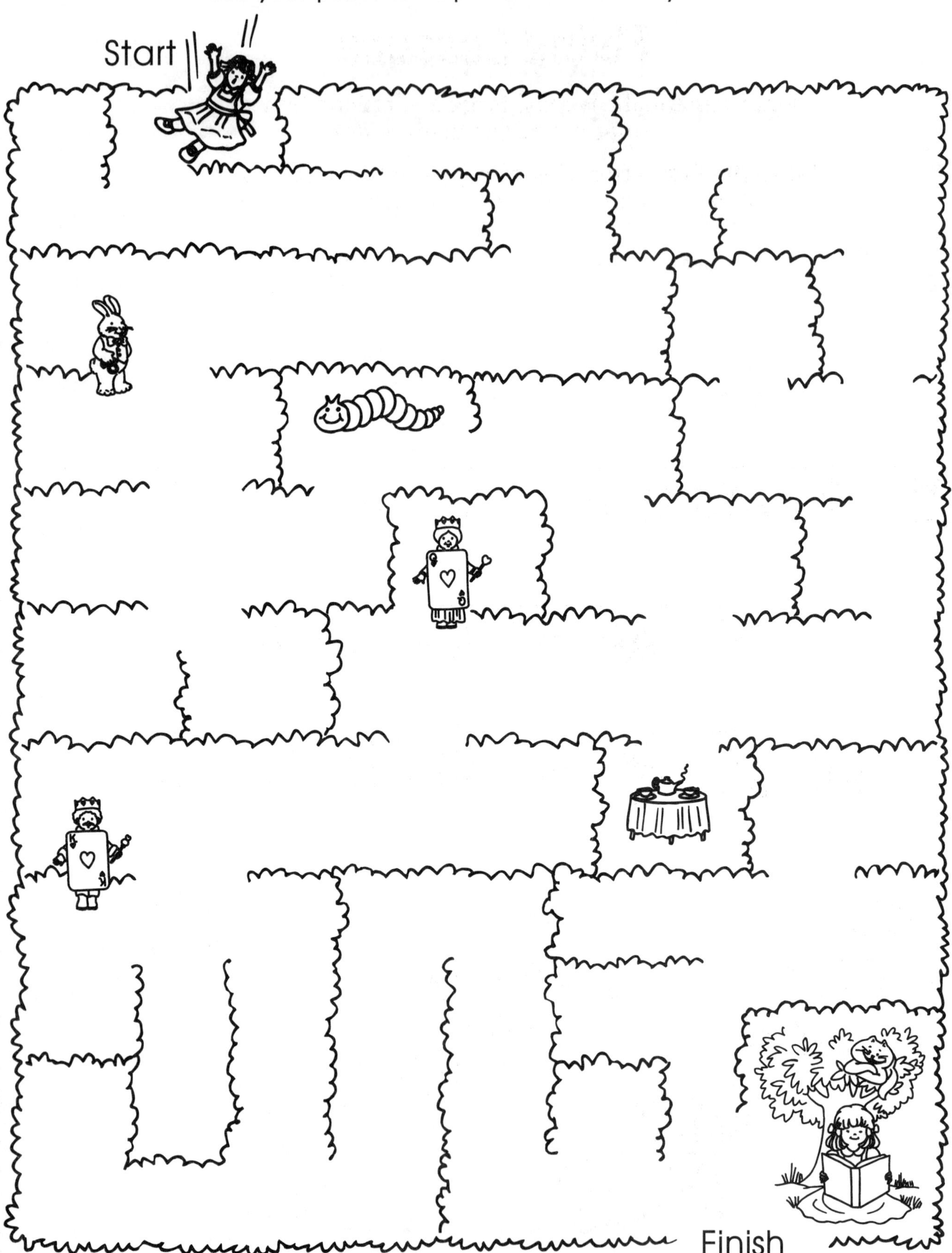

Flying Lessons

Peter Pan taught Wendy, Michael and John how to fly.
What did he tell them to do?

Write the first letter of each object in the space above it.
When you are done, you will have the answer.

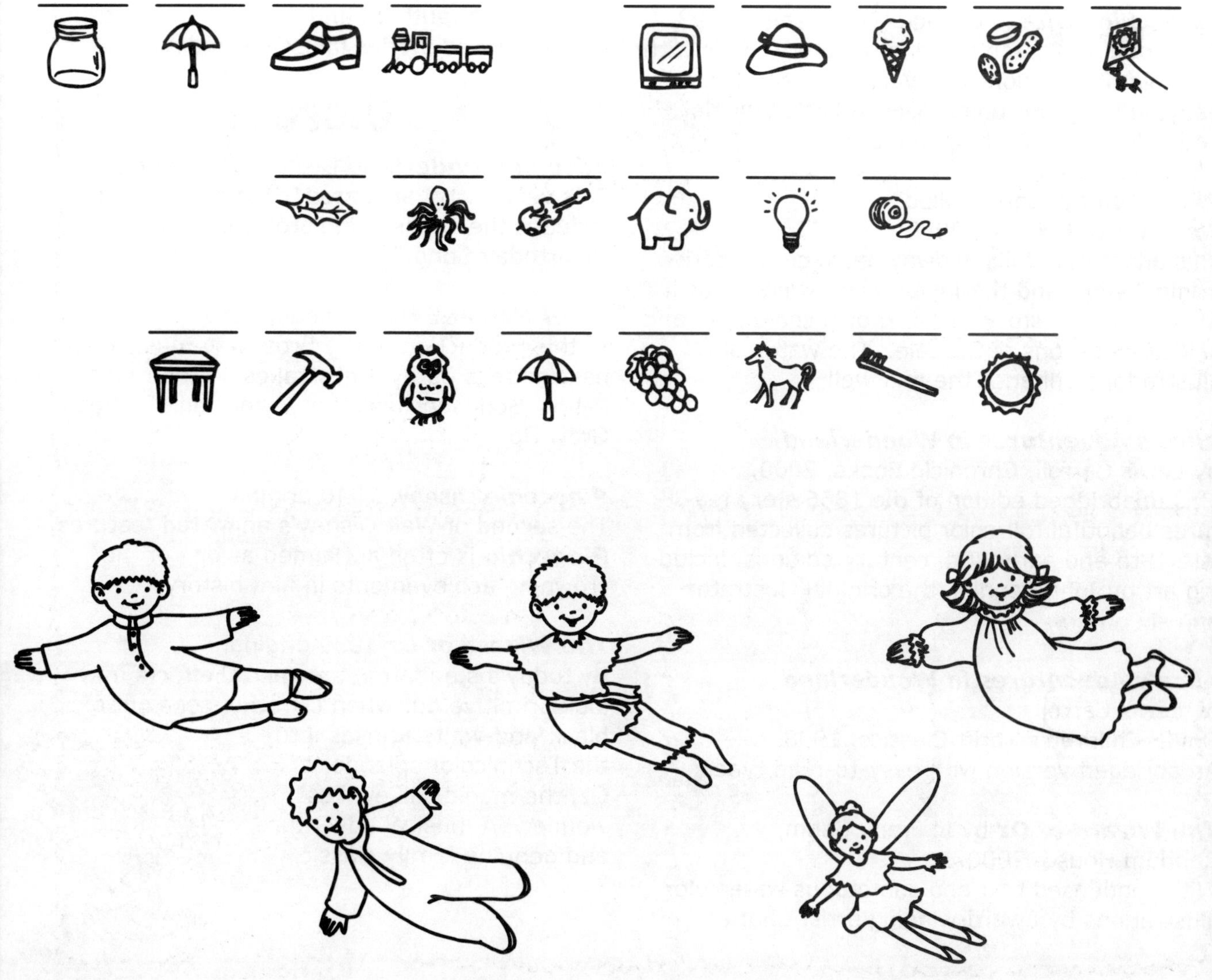

The Books & Media

Classic Tales Books

Paperback and hardcover editions of the four classic tales are available in every library and bookstore. While it is always preferable to read each story in its original version, the vocabulary and length can be off-putting for younger readers. The versions listed here are notable for the abridged texts, the quality of the illustrations or other unique assets.

Peter Pan by Sir James Barrie,
Golden Books, 1995.
With illustrations and vocabulary geared to ages 4-8, this version is well suited for primary grade readers.

Peter Pan by Sir James Barrie,
Chronicle Books, 2000.
The outstanding illustrations by different artists make this edition a pleasure to share with children.

Pinocchio by Carlo Collodi, Walt Disney, 1993.
This book and cassette bring the story to life with full-color illustrations on every page and accompanying songs including "Give a Little Whistle" and "When You Wish upon a Star."

Pinocchio by Carlo Collodi,
Wordsworth Editions, 2000.
This adaptation falls midway between the dark original story and the joyful Disney version as it focuses on the story's best-known characters and selected portions of the tale. The watercolor illustrations enhance the text well.

Alice's Adventures in Wonderland
by Lewis Carroll, Chronicle Books, 2000.
This unabridged edition of the 1866 story features beautiful full-color pictures collected from late 19th and early 20th century editions, including art by John Tenniel, the original illustrator and six others.

Alice's Adventures in Wonderland
by Lewis Carroll,
Dover Children's Thrift Classics, 1998.
An abridged version with easy-to-read type.

The Wizard of Oz by L. Frank Baum,
Random House, 2000.
With condensed text and sumptuous watercolor illustrations by award-winning artist Charles Santore on every page, this edition is highly recommended for young readers.

***The Wonderful Wizard of Oz:
A Commemorative Pop-Up***
by L. Frank Baum, Little Simon, 2000.
In this resplendent version, a spinning tornado, waving poppies, sparkling touches of colored foil, Emerald City eyeglasses and other pop-up features captivate young and old. A tour de force of paper engineering and a stunning work of art.

The Wizard of Oz 100th Anniversary Edition
by L. Frank Baum, Henry Holt, 2000.
Brilliant pictures, large type and brief biographies of the author and Michael Hague, the book's well-known illustrator, enrich the classic story.

Oz: The Hundredth Anniversary Celebration
HarperCollins, 2000.
Find out how the tales of Oz enchanted and influenced Eric Carle, Tomie de Paola, Chris Van Allsburg and 27 other authors and artists who pay tribute to the beloved stories in essays and pictures.

Videos

Alice in Wonderland Disney, 1951 original.
This very pretty animated, dream-like movie includes the songs "I'm Late" and "The Unbirthday Song."

Peter Pan A&E Home Video, 1997.
In this production of the Broadway musical, gymnast/actress Cathy Rigby takes on the role of Peter. Songs include "I'm Flying" and "I Won't Grow Up."

Pinocchio Disney, 1940 original.
The second of Walt Disney's animated features, ***Pinocchio*** is often acclaimed as one of the crowning achievements in film history.

The Wizard of Oz 1939 original
By today's standards, the special effects may look primitive but when Dorothy steps out of black-and-white Kansas into the Technicolor splendor of Oz, the magic still evokes wonder. A musical adventure and genuine family classic.

The Snack

Over the Rainbow
Fruit Salad

Ask parents to contribute fruit for this colorful and healthy rainbow salad. To create the rainbow, you'll need the following fruits, either fresh, canned or frozen and thawed.

Red–strawberries, watermelon, cherries, raspberries
Orange–cantaloupe, oranges, apricots
Yellow–pineapple, bananas
Green–honeydew, kiwi, green grapes
Blue–blueberries
Purple–purple grapes, plums

- Wash and peel fruit and then cut into bite-size pieces or cubes.

- On a large tray or platter, arrange the red fruit to create the top arch of the rainbow.

- Follow with the orange fruit below the red, then add the remaining fruit in order–yellow, green, blue and purple.

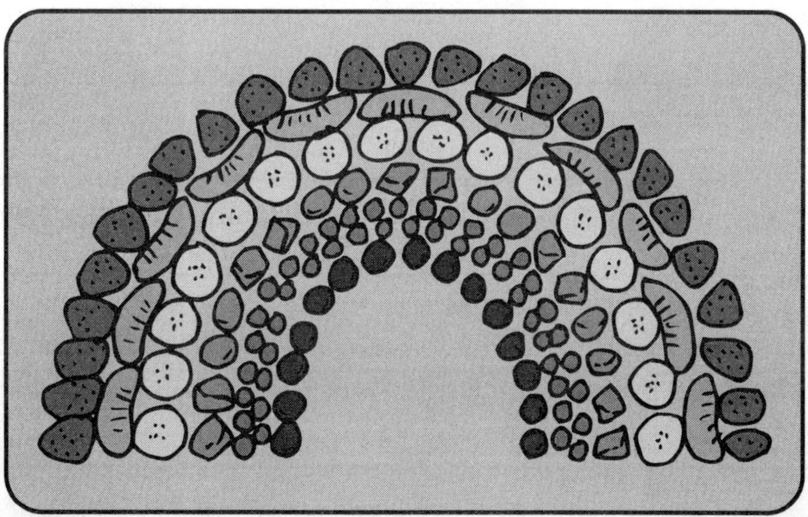

For an additional treat, make a "yellow brick road" using vanilla wafers. Place a tablecloth on a table and have children arrange the wafers in the shape of a winding road.

The Clip Art

The Clip Art

The Reproducibles

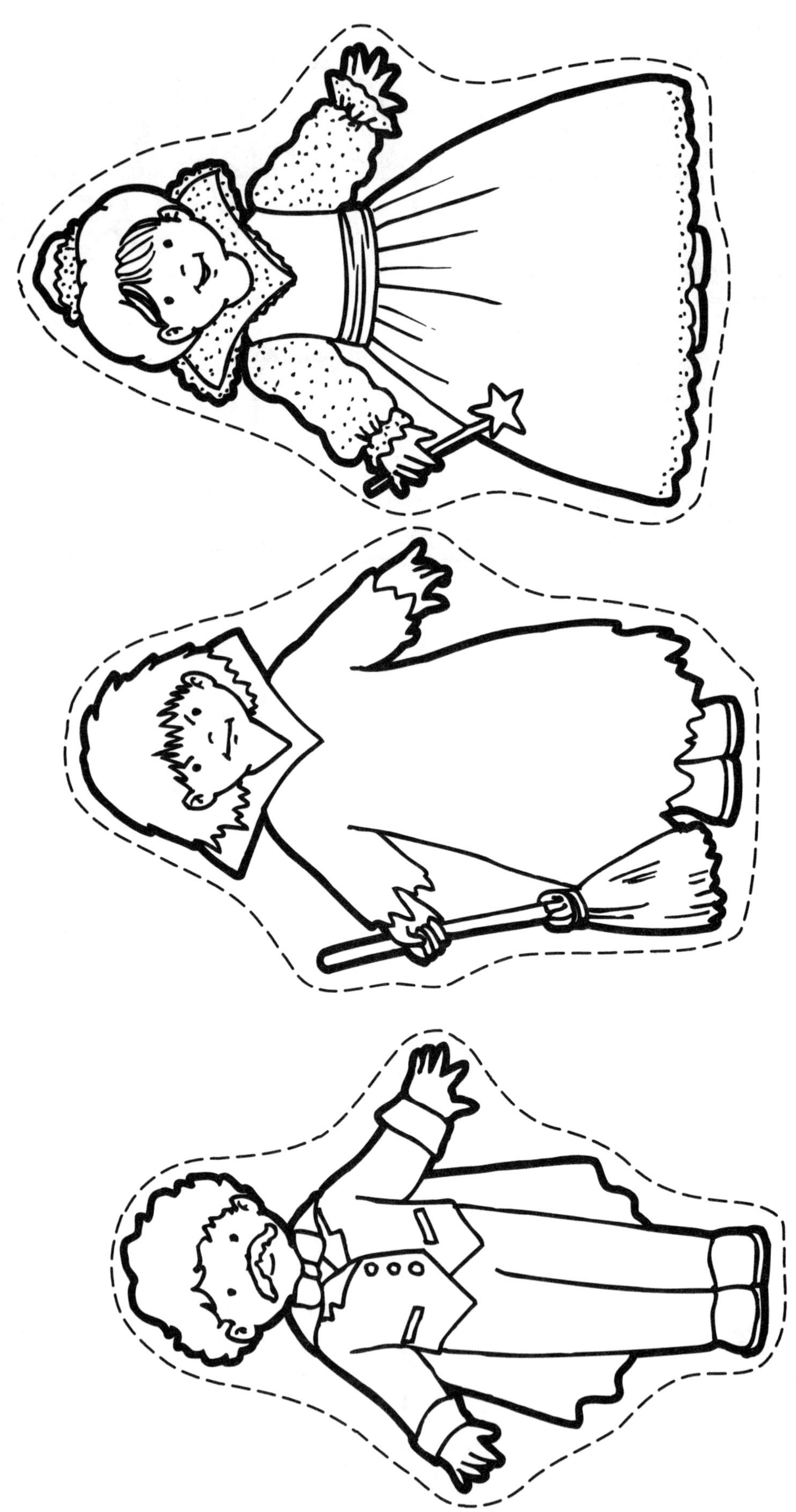

Follow the yellow brick road to

___________________'s

room.

We're hooked on books!

The Reproducibles

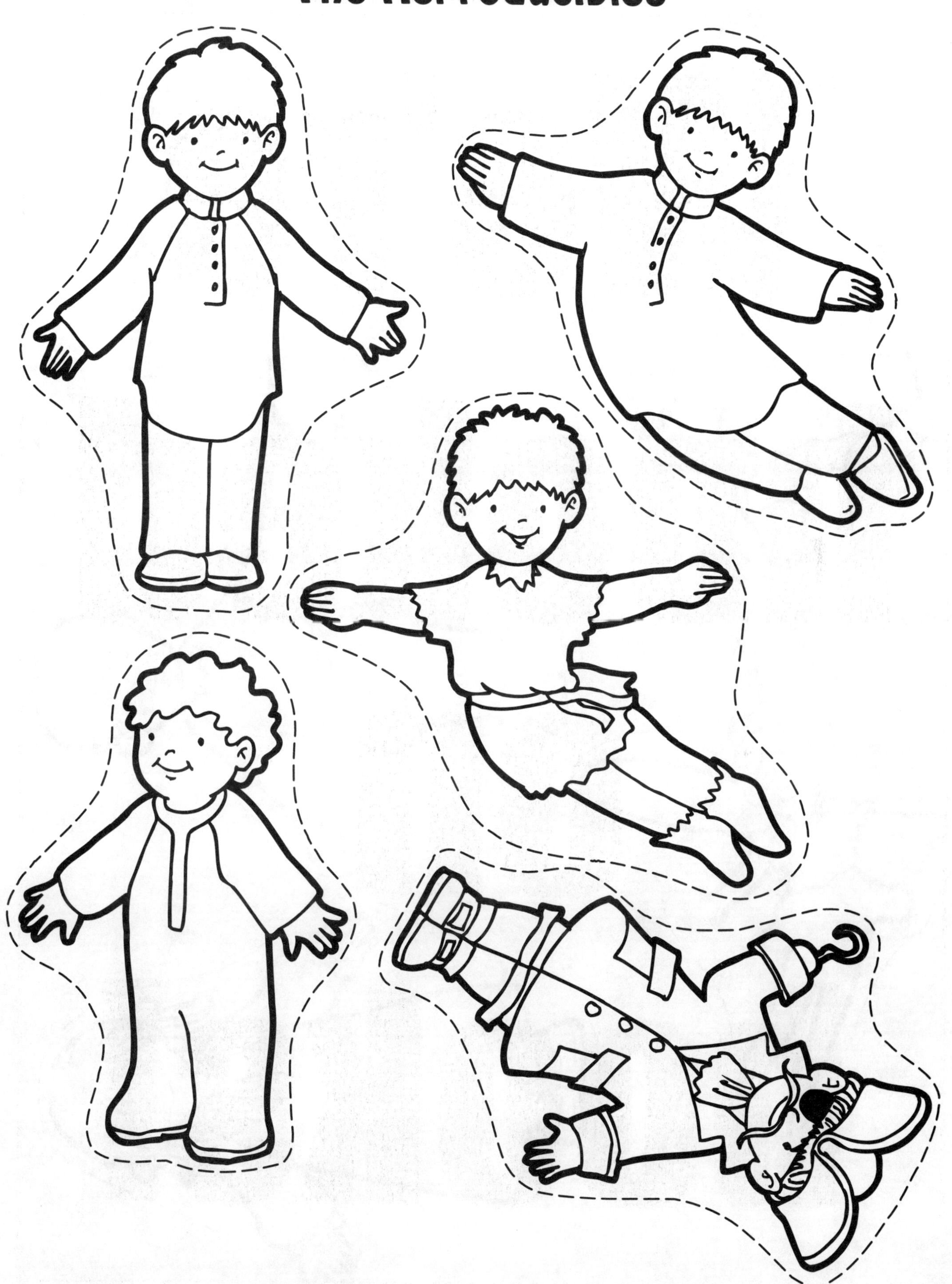

The Reproducibles

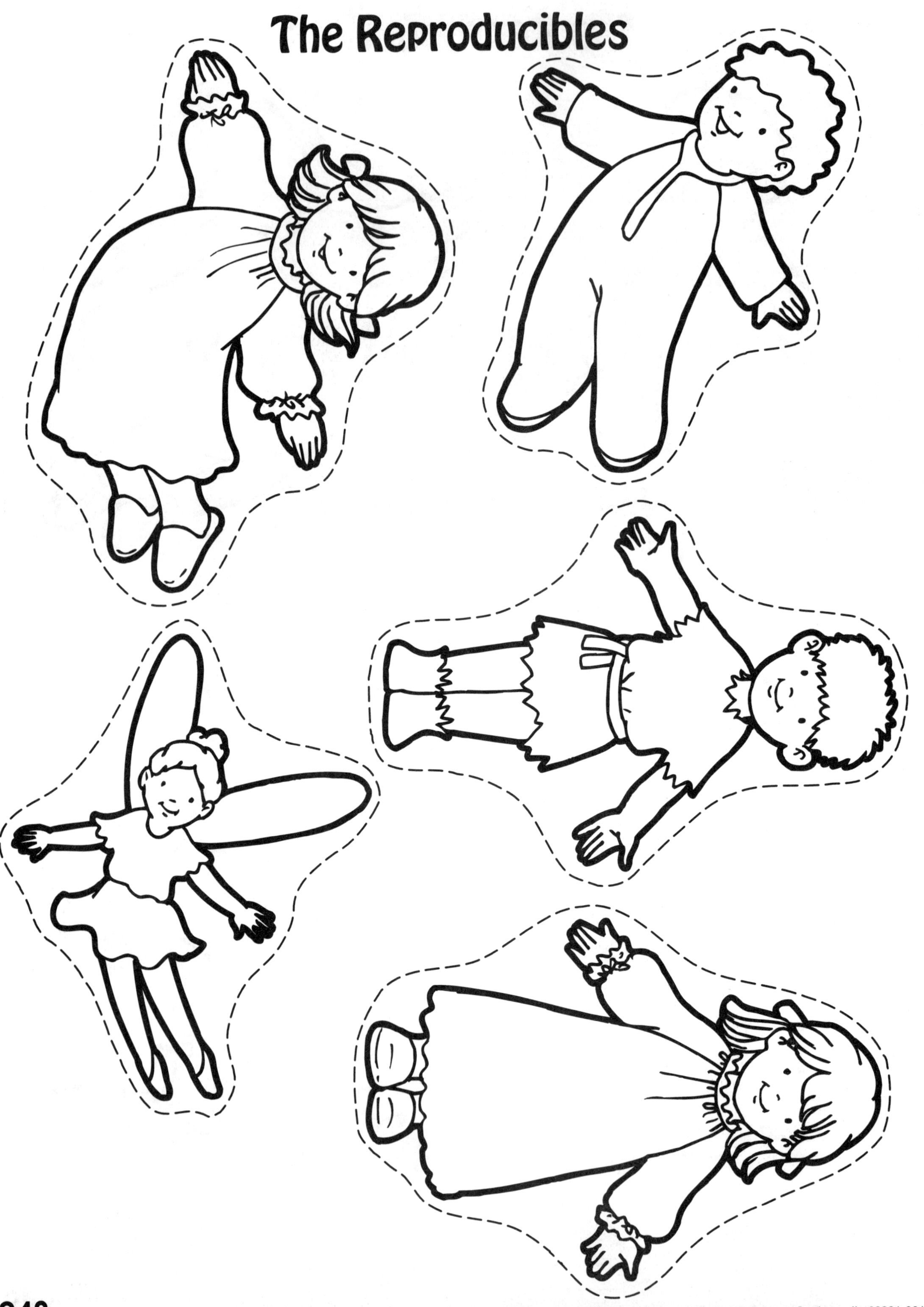

Mad Math Tea Party

The Reproducibles

Reproducibles

Don't be like Pinocchio,
Here are safety rules
you should know:

Today's

Helpers

Once upon a time ...

And they lived happily ever after.

The Reproducibles

The Reproducibles